Of Passion and Folly

A Scriptural Foundation for Peace

Patricia McCarthy, C.N.D.

A Liturgical Press Book

THE LITURGICAL PRESS
Collegeville, Minnesota

Cover design by Fred Petters. Illustration: *The Return of the Prodigal Son,* Rembrandt, ca. 1642.

The Scripture quotations are from the New Revised Standard Version Bible, Catholic edition, © 1989 by the Division of Christian Education of the National Council of Churches of Christ in the USA. Used by permission. All rights reserved.

1	2	3	4	5	6	7	8

Library of Congress Cataloging-in-Publication Data

McCarthy, Patricia, 1944–
    Of passion and folly : a scriptural foundation for peace / Patricia McCarthy.
        p.   cm.
    Includes bibliographical references.
    ISBN 0-8146-2469-3 (alk. paper)
    1. Peace–Religious aspects–Christianity.   2. Christian life–Catholic authors.   I. Title.
BT736.4.M38   1998
261.8'.73–dc21   97-41222
                                           CIP

Because your steadfast love is
better than life,
my lips will praise you
(Ps 63:3).

*To my mother and father
and
to the memory of Fr. Marty Jenco who proclaimed
by his life that,
"The words of Jesus need no defense."*

CONTENTS

PREFACE

Usually books are written to clarify ideas, express opinions, or propose theories. This book is being written to raise questions and to encourage participation in living out the process of answering them. The questions are: Why is peace simultaneously so desirable and so unimportant? Can we seek the goal of peace while avoiding the means of peace? Is peace an option or a tenet of our faith?

Peace seems to be desired if we listen to the constant cry for the cessation of wars and for the return of safety and security to our homes and streets. People pray for peace; they bemoan the daily log of killings and assaults. The elderly and the young, sick and healthy, rich and poor—all want peace. Dictators and oppressors claim they want peace. Victims of unjust regimes and refugees of war want peace. While the precise terms for peace and the meaning of peace vary, the desire is constant.

Universal as is the desire for peace, it doesn't seem important to most of us. Is this a contradiction? Perhaps. Or perhaps it simply clarifies what our desires really are. Importance is a measurable attribute. The priority or value we give anything can be measured by the time, effort, and commitment of resources we invest in it. According to these standards, peace doesn't seem to be a high priority.

We want peaceful homes, but what efforts do we put into making that happen? We complain about the violence on

television and in the movies, yet we continue to expose ourselves to it. We worry about the violence in our children's
lives, yet we buy toys that foster it. We disapprove of the
greed and fierce competition in professional sports, but we
still support them. We seem disturbed by the slaughter of innocent people around the world, but we spend more than
half of our tax money on the production and maintenance of
the military machine. Our actions are sometimes inconsistent
with our desires. We want peace yet we rarely step into the
way of peace.

The intent of this book is to help us question the reality
of how we live and measure it against the scriptures. This
book will not transform reality, but our response to the Word
of God will. Conversion to God's ways can move us from
merely desiring peace to deliberately choosing peace. The
basis of our choice is awareness of our call to peace, a call
given us in Baptism, strengthened in Confirmation, renewed
in confession, and nourished in Eucharist. Union with the
one who came among us as the Prince of Peace is the goal of
a life of peace.

To reach that goal we set our sights on Christ and train
and strain until we reach him. "Do you not know that in a
race all the runners compete, but only one receives the prize?
Run in such a way that you may win it. Athletes exercise self-
control in all things; they do it to receive a perishable wreath,
but we an imperishable one" (1 Cor 9:24-25).

A runner cannot run only on race day. Training and
preparation of months and years can go into a single race.
Gospel living also takes training and preparation. In this
book, each chapter is followed by a reflective prayer/response
suggestion. Readers are encouraged to contemplate the scriptures into action, to let the gospel of Christ become the light
of peace in our violence-darkened world.

Breaking through this cover of war, oppression, revenge,
hatred, and injustice, the Incarnate Light penetrates us, opening us to the divine command: "Love one another as I have

loved you." Splitting the atom is less difficult than shattering society's presumption that such peace-producing love is impossible. This kind of love becomes a threat to personal or national interests. This kind of love includes those who hurt, cheat, rape, kill, ignore, starve, or imprison us. "Love your enemies and pray for those who persecute you." Beyond feelings, beyond fears, beyond human potential, beyond imagination, the Word of God calls.

Jesus' words are clear. He calls for a radical, all-consuming love of each other as the means to peace. The words of Jesus need no defense. If we keep them before us, we will become peace in our time as Jesus was in Jerusalem two thousand years ago when the passion of his love was nailed to the folly of the cross. In that union abides peace.

Chapter One

NOT A NEW THEOLOGY

As Christians we know that all things begin in Christ, so we begin the journey of peace in Christ. We look at Christ, we listen to Christ, we walk with Christ, we live with Christ, and we die with Christ. This is the theology of peace.

It is a theology which is defined by love and expressed by nonviolence. Christic love is not one aspect of peace; it is the essence of it. We cannot separate Christ from his message. The precepts he left us are our moral code and spiritual guide, and the example he gave us is our standard and inspiration. To understand the word of peace we begin with the Word of God–Jesus.

Jesus Christ was born of a woman who was a member of the chosen people at a time in their history when they were politically oppressed. Thus Jesus started life on this earth positioned between the intimacy of the covenant and the vulnerability of powerlessness. But this Jesus Christ is also God; and if this juxtaposition of mercy and misery was the situation into which he chose to be born, then it deserves our attention and consideration. To walk with Jesus of Nazareth, to hear him speak from the fullness of God's covenant with humanity, we must understand something of this covenant.

Jesus: Born into a covenant of intimacy

The Hebrew people lived by the covenant God formed with them over generations.

> Now therefore, if you obey my voice and keep my covenant, you shall be my treasured possession out of all the peoples (Exod 19:5).

They were God's people, the chosen ones.

> I have made a covenant with my chosen one (Ps 89:3).

God, in all power and might, reached into the heart of a people in pain, darkness, and misery; God restored hope with the touch of gentle healing, infinite light, and tender mercy. As we see from the covenant with Israel, in both its inception and its lived reality, covenant is a call. God initiates and seduces and then awaits the return of love as an excuse for more love. To those who hear the call, experience the security of acceptance, and feel the stirrings of desire, God offers the covenant which demands all their heart and soul. For those who allow themselves to be seduced, Yahweh becomes their God. They fall in love with the Almighty One.

> O LORD, God of Israel, there is no God like you in heaven above or on earth beneath, keeping covenant and steadfast love for your servants who walk before you with all their heart (1 Kgs 8:23).

This covenant tradition was not one of contract but of relationship. God entered into a bond of love with *all* the Hebrew people, even while expressing it through specific individuals. God loved Noah and Abraham, Moses and Miriam, Isaac and Jacob, Judith and Esther, Tobit and Ruth, Rebecca and Joseph. And through them God loved *all* their friends and families and children. The community of chosen people knew the love of God for all through the unique and intimate love experienced by many individuals. From the beginning it has been the way of God to embrace all by loving one by one, thus linking forever the individual with the community. There can be no friendship with God apart from the community of brothers and sisters.

By focusing on just this aspect of covenant—the relationship between the individual and the community—it becomes obvious that covenant is never static or permanently fixed, as, for instance, a family heirloom handed down from parents to children and grandchildren. The covenant indeed passes through generations but it is always new and always dependent upon response.

> Not with our ancestors did the LORD make this covenant,
> but with us, who are all of us here alive today (Deut 5:3).

Our love for each other is the critical measure of our commitment to the covenant. After all, entering into a relationship of love is not just an emotional experience. Commitment is the fuel which keeps the spirit afire long after feelings have waned. Responsibility accompanies relationship. God promises to be faithful from generation to generation, yet those chosen must strive for their own fidelity as well. Response is crucial in keeping relationships viable and active throughout the highs and lows of daily life. The hands of love willingly embrace the ongoing struggle between law and spirit, freedom and accountability, control and powerlessness. It is this very struggle which forges the chains of love that bind us in covenant to God.

Even sin is no excuse for severing the bond since mercy and forgiveness dwell eternally in the heart of God. In covenant God demands such a torrent of love that it will rush through our lives, crashing over obstacles of fear and weakness.

Physical expressions of covenant

Appropriately, such an exacting covenant was ritualized in the flesh. The Hebrews sealed their covenant with the living

God with the flesh of the males, foreshadowing a future covenant sealed with the flesh of the living God in Jesus Christ. Circumcision was the identifiable and irreversible mark of commitment. It was the physical reminder of the real mark of the covenant which was the surrender of one's whole being. Only in Jesus can we understand the depth of the surrender, but its call was there from the beginning.

The great cry for the Sabbath Day was another physical expression of the covenant with God. To render God the Sabbath did not mean merely giving God one day of prayer; it meant giving God one's life. Legalism interpreted attendance at temple service to be the fulfillment of the commandment to "Keep holy the Sabbath Day." But that was never the original intent of the precept for the ancient Jews, just as it is not the intent of the contemporary commandment to participate in Eucharist every week. To give God the Sabbath is to worship God alone; and worship presupposes putting God first in every detail and decision of our lives. To keep holy the Sabbath is to surrender to the Holy every moment of every day—from sunrise to sunset, from sunset to sunrise.

Covenant of peace for all

Just as the covenant was never meant to be celebrated only one day of the week, so also God's all-embracing covenant was never intended to be exclusively for the Israelites. They were simply the ones through whom the message would be carried to everyone else. And the message to be carried was one of fidelity, mercy, and peace.

> For the mountains may depart and the hills be removed, but my steadfast love shall not depart from you, and my covenant of peace shall not be removed, says the LORD, who has compassion on you (Isa 54:10).

> I will make with them a covenant of peace and banish wild animals from the land, so that they may live in the wild and sleep in the woods securely (Ezek 34:25).

I will make for you a covenant on that day with the wild animals, the birds of the air, and the creeping things of the ground; and I will abolish the bow, the sword, and war from the land; and I will make you lie down in safety (Hos 2:18).

My covenant with him [Levi] was one of life and wellbeing (Mal 2:5).

From the beginning the call for peace was clearly an integral part of the covenant. Yet the history of God's covenanted people often resounds with the shouts and cries of battle. It is inconsistent with the message of the covenant. But the inconsistency is due to the weakness of the people not the inadequacy of the covenant itself. Peace has always been integral to relationship with God. And the cry for peace has always been aroused in the human heart by the touch of God.

Jesus: Prince of Peace born into oppression

Is there ever a more poignant cry for peace than that which comes from the depths of unrest and violence? The most passionate pleas for peace come from those suffering war; the most intense longing for freedom comes from those in chains. Jesus was born into the covenant which promised peace when those chosen to carry the covenant were under Roman domination, suffering political oppression.

There were many times in the history of God's people when the Hebrews were free and secure. They had their time of earthly glory under David and Solomon. They had security while Joseph sat close to the Pharaoh in Egypt. They had the political victories of Esther over Ahasuerus and Judith over Holofernes. Moses freed them from Egyptian tyranny; and during their desert wandering they were not under a foreign yoke.

Jesus' time was not such a one. Rome ruled all of Israel, and the people suffered from the changeable whims of the emperor and his appointed kings and governors. There was no democracy, justice, or security. All the characteristics of oppression were present in the daily routines of the people: poverty, fear, torture, executions, injustice, separation of families.

Into this vacuum of societal freedom Jesus was born. By his birth Jesus showed that the absence or presence of human power was immaterial to the covenant. God would be faithful; the people would be fortified and redeemed. Rome, in its illusion of power and control, had no effect whatsoever on the fulfillment of the promises of God.[1] No earthly power could interfere with, impede, or advance the coming of the kingdom.

Let us be very clear that God in Jesus was not indifferent to the pain of the people. Justice is the foundation of the kingdom, and injustice is a defilement of the ways of God. And justice for God can only be the fruit of love. Power cannot be conquered by greater power but only by a love which eagerly embraces powerlessness for the sake of the Beloved.

What God revealed about the kingdom at the time of the Hebrew prophets and what God spoke through Jesus, God still speaks today. Jesus used no force, gained no political power, suffered rejection, and redeemed us by being nailed naked to a cross—a position of ultimate vulnerability. Such vulnerability is both a prerequisite and a fruit of the presence of God among the people. In his body, Jesus showed us the marks of the covenant—total openness to the throes of passion whatever the personal cost.

The marks of the covenant will be the same for us. Vulnerability is the sign of God's kingdom upon earth; force and intimidation are not. They are wasteful realities and have nothing in common with the ways of God.

Jesus Christ knew the ways of God and lived his life in obedience to the will of God. Jesus Christ and the Father are one; the union is perfect. On the strength of this intimacy, Jesus, while on this earth, could resist the temptation to operate according to the false standards of control and power. Jesus could risk powerlessness because he dwelt in the embrace of God from which no one could take him. Jesus knew covenant intimately and trusted in it explicitly. It was the intimacy of the covenant which gave Jesus the strength to embrace the powerlessness of it. It will be the same for us. Union with God will give us the courage to be vulnerable in our love for God and for one another. Positioned between intimacy and vulnerability we will be ready to be people of peace.

Covenant

I have made a covenant with my chosen one (Ps 89:3).

Now therefore, if you obey my voice and keep my covenant, you shall be my treasured possession out of all the peoples (Exod 19:5).

O LORD, God of Israel, there is no God like you in heaven above or on earth beneath, keeping covenant and steadfast love for your servants who walk before you with all their heart (1Kgs 8:23).

Not with our ancestors did the LORD make this covenant, but with us, who are all of us here alive today (Deut 5:3).

For the mountains may depart and the hills be removed, but my steadfast love shall not depart from you, and my covenant of peace shall not be removed, says the LORD, who has compassion on you (Isa 54:10).

I will make with them a covenant of peace and banish wild animals from the land, so that they may live in the wild and sleep in the woods securely (Ezek 34:25).

1. Acknowledge the presence of God. Ask for the light of the Spirit during this time of prayer.

2. Read the Scripture passages on covenant and choose one which attracts you.
3. Read slowly the passage you have chosen three times. Hear God speaking these words to you personally.
4. Reflect on the face of God as revealed in this passage.
5. In the presence of God read the same passage slowly three more times. This time hear yourself speaking the words to God.
6. Reflect on your own identity as revealed in this passage.
7. Now compare what this passage reveals about God and about yourself. Are you in covenant with each other? How is the covenant expressed in your daily life? How can this covenant be renewed?
8. Close this prayer with the song of Moses:

> The LORD is my strength and my might, and he has become my salvation; this is my God, and I will praise him. . . . (Exod 15:2).

Chapter Two

DECISIONS FOR PEACE

It is in his life on this earth that we see Jesus giving flesh to the concepts of intimacy and powerlessness, the cornerstone of his theology of peace. Sometimes it is easier to understand through example than precept as attempts at clarification become simplified in the light of living proof. So we need to walk with Jesus as he begins his active ministry in Galilee. God has become human and is about to show us what it means to live as a child of God. We will see the theology of peace in action.

We begin following Jesus as he prepares for his apostolate of preaching, teaching, and healing. Jesus meets John who is baptizing by the River Jordan. John announces Jesus as the Lamb of God, the One for whom John has been preparing the people. Jesus and John were cousins; their mothers were friends, so the two young men knew each other. Surely John had heard the story about their meeting while both were still in their mothers' wombs. Elizabeth and Zachariah must have related to John the stories of his birth and Jesus' birth.

John's reaction to Jesus was to announce him to the crowd as the Messiah and to try to step aside. The confusion comes when Jesus asks to be baptized. John protests because he knows Jesus is the Chosen One of God. John is right when he confesses that he is unworthy for such a responsibility. Jesus gently insists, "Let it be so now; for it is proper for us in this way to fulfill all righteousness" (Matt 3:15).

Though sinless Jesus submitted to a symbolic baptism to fulfill the plan of God, an act of obedient worship that brought the voice of God to Jordan's banks.

"This is my Son, the Beloved, with whom I am well pleased" (Matt 3:17).

God could not contain the love of Father for Son; the people must know how great is this love.

For anyone who risks embracing the theology of peace this is our starting point as it was for Jesus in his public life. We stand before God allowing the waters of life to pour over us and giving God the opportunity to pronounce over us the words said to Jesus. Each of us hears God proclaiming: "This is my beloved son, this is my beloved daughter in whom I am well pleased."

Standing in the presence of God, confident of the love of God, we experience the first phase of being a peacemaker—an abiding sense of God's deep acceptance and intimate love for us.

Christians who hide under a false humility with claims of unworthiness are not being faithful to such a covenant of blessings. Obviously no one is worthy of or has a right to God's love; but God wants us to know we are loved. How else can we surrender to God unless we are sure God desires us and takes pleasure in us? If we don't have knowledge of God's love for us, we need to stay with Jesus by the Jordan until we receive it. It is futile to try to understand the rest of Jesus' actions and words apart from the experience of being loved by God. It is necessary to know we are loved before we can hear the call of the gospel.

There is little danger here of slipping into an exclusively "God and me" idea of religion. Once we hear God speaking intimately to us we realize not only our own worth in God's eyes but also the worth of others. When we acknowledge God's delight in us personally, we also acknowledge God's delight in each of our brothers and sisters. We hear God's litany:

"This is my beloved Jesus,
this is my beloved John,
this is my beloved Mary,
this is my beloved Hinako,
this is my beloved Charles,
this is my beloved Mairead,
this is my beloved Mohammad,
this is my beloved Kirsten,
this is my beloved Takisha,
this is my beloved Magda,
this is my beloved Antonio."

No person, no race, no faith, no country is excluded from the love of God. We are all God's beloved children, invited to union with the Almighty.

Jesus risking the desert

For so intimate a call the response must be that of vulnerability. Jesus hears God's words of love and is immediately led into the desert, the place of vulnerability. Jesus goes into the wilderness to struggle with power and its illusions; prayer and fasting are his only defenses. Jesus has to make decisions that will determine immediately his course of action and ultimately his death. He takes the risk because he is sure of the love and because he believes in his mission.

It is in the desert that Jesus shows his determination to be faithful to God's mission of bringing the kingdom of God to earth. These decisions of Jesus, forged from the experience of temptation, are important for us so that we may come to recognize the ways of God in our own work of bringing the kingdom to our times.

First temptation

> Then Jesus was led up by the Spirit into the wilderness to
> be tempted by the devil. He fasted forty days and forty
> nights, and afterwards he was famished. The tempter
> came and said to him, "If you are the Son of God, com-
> mand these stones to become loaves of bread." But he an-
> swered, "It is written: 'One does not live by bread alone,
> but by every word that comes from the mouth of God'"
> (Matt 4:1-4).

In the first temptation Jesus resists economic power, a
power which makes us look good before others. The goal of
Jesus' mission is not to feed and heal and console; the goal is
to praise God. Turning stones into bread isn't the mission of
Jesus; living on the word of God is. Jesus isn't denouncing
the works of mercy but he is clarifying that, as important as
they are, they are not the goal. They are a sign of the presence of God but they are not God.

In practical terms this temptation is not as easy to resist
as it is simple to understand. Only those who have lived side
by side with the poor and oppressed know how serious is the
temptation to do anything to relieve their sufferings, even if
it involves picking up the gun of violent revolution, accepting
financial assistance from corrupt sources or killing others in
order to stop them from killing the innocent. To refuse participation in evil when the immediate result looks helpful is
to stand vulnerable in a desert of despair, trusting in the ways
of God even when they seem useless. Jesus said "no" and, in
his strength, we say "no." This denial of economic power as
the goal of the kingdom allows us the opportunity to declare
ourselves people of God, not of this world.

Second temptation

> Then the devil took him to the holy city and placed him on
> the pinnacle of the temple, saying to him, "If you are the
> Son of God, throw yourself down; for it is written: 'He will

command his angels concerning you,' and 'On their hands they will bear you up, so that you will not dash your foot against a stone.'" Jesus said to him, "Again it is written, 'Do not put the Lord your God to the test'" (Matt 4:5-7).

Jesus' next temptation flows from the first. If he refuses economic power he is also giving up political power. He is surrendering control and again assuming the posture of a poor person. The poor have no control over much that affects their lives. If they don't like their neighborhood, they can't move. If they have inferior schools, they can't afford private ones. If they are sick they can't get to the medical specialists. A loss of control over life can lead to a rage of bitterness and revenge or an abyss of hopelessness. Jesus leads us down a difficult road when he severs his ties to the glory and convenience of control.

This temptation to control is not subtle: "Throw yourself down and call on the angels to catch you." Being in control creates an aura of power. Jesus could command attention if he had angels at his bidding. But that is not why Jesus came. Again his answer is simple: "Don't put God to the test." God is God. Jesus shows us that it is not our place to decide how God is to act in any situation. We are not God; we cannot manipulate God; and we cannot assume the control over life that belongs only to God. Abandonment is Jesus' passionate dismissal of control.

How foolish, according to the world's standards, is such a position! The meek never get anywhere. The Christian does not need to get anywhere. "To dwell in the house of the LORD all days" is sufficient. The glory of political power holds no sway over the heart surrendered to God.

Third temptation

Again, the devil took him to a very high mountain and showed him all the kingdoms of the world and their splendor; and he said to him, "All these I will give you, if you will fall down and worship me." Jesus said to him, "Away with you, Satan! for it is written, 'Worship the Lord your God, and serve only him'" (Matt 4:8-10).

Jesus' final temptation is to idolatry. "Here are all the kingdoms of the world. Take them—just do so at the expense of denying God." This is the temptation to spiritual power. For the sake of religion we take on the practices of the devil. The end justifies the means. In the Middle Ages, we formed crusades "to rescue the Holy Land from the infidel." In the name of God we killed our brother and sister Muslims. Today, we often ignore the human rights of many for the well-being of a few because the wealthy are more important to the future of the Church than the nameless poor. Sometimes we are just too comfortable in our faith to let the Word of God stir us from apathy. We keep silent about injustice lest we lose our influence in the community and endanger the good standing of the Church. Perhaps if we disagree too much with governmental policies the Church in the United States might lose its tax-exempt status.

Our clinging to false securities is a form of idolatry. To resist the third temptation, as Jesus did, is to smash the idols and to be freed of the false hopes and fickle standards that ensnare us. The hardest part of resisting this temptation is recognizing it as a temptation. We don't admit to idolatry when ambition for advancement, greed for material possessions, or armed defense for security reasons block out the living God. We don't see ourselves as denying God; we just aren't used to thinking God has anything to do with our personal, social, or business life. God belongs only in church!

These three temptations build on each other. If we give in to the first and base our decisions and set our goals on money and economic power, we blind ourselves to even recognizing the second temptation to political power. When making money is accepted as a priority, political power follows without any further choices on our part. If both of these temptations are not resisted then the one to idolatry is never even felt. We just slip into it. Money and power have already become idols, and God has been confined to a limited sphere of influence in our lives.

God is always God and can break through any wall of defense, no matter how solidly we have constructed it. But God will never force love and, if we must "be of love (a little) more careful than of everything,"[2] then we must be very careful to take seriously the inner struggles we experience. We must see them as occasions for choice and growth that will open the door to greater choices and deeper growth in the future. All will lead, as it did in Jesus, to confidence in the presence of God and commitment for the mission of God.

> Then the devil left him, and suddenly angels came and waited on him (Matt. 4:11).

Jesus left the desert in the presence of angels and began his ministry of actively bringing the kingdom of God to the people. We leave our desert places vulnerable and free, and we begin our lives as disciples of Jesus and proclaimers of the good news. The angels of God accompany, guide and protect us, and the presence of God envelops us.

Decisions for Peace: An Examination of Conscience

1. Be aware of the presence of Christ who faced temptations.
2. Ask for the grace of honesty. Pray for clarity of heart before him.

First Temptation

> Then Jesus was led up by the Spirit into the wilderness to be tempted by the devil. He fasted forty days and forty nights, and afterwards he was famished. The tempter came and said to him, "If you are the Son of

God, command these stones to become loaves of bread."
But he answered, "It is written: 'One does not live by
bread alone, but by every word that comes from the
mouth of God'" (Matt 4:1-4).

1. Is money a god in my life?
2. Do I share my financial resources with the poor?
3. Do I support the church where I worship?
4. Do I sacrifice time with my family in the pursuit of financial gain?
5. Do I judge others by their standard of living?
6. Is my standard of living consistent with the gospel?
7. Do I despair over the lack of money in my life?
8. Am I greedy?
9. Is money more important to me than friendship?
10. Are financial disagreements a source of conflict among family, friends, and business associates?
11. Do I give my employees a decent wage?
12. Am I honest in all financial dealings?

Second Temptation

Then the devil took him to the holy city and placed him on
the pinnacle of the temple, saying to him, "If you are the
Son of God, throw yourself down; for it is written: 'He will
command his angels concerning you,' and 'On their hands
they will bear you up, so that you will not dash your foot
against a stone.'" Jesus said to him, "Again it is written, 'Do
not put the Lord your God to the test'" (Matt 4:5-7).

1. Have I ever consciously surrendered to God the details of my life?
2. Can I wait in line patiently?
3. Do I try to get my way whenever there is a disagreement?
4. Do I get angry at people when I don't get my way?

5. Am I patient with others' weaknesses?
6. Do I drive my car in peace or in anger at other drivers?
7. Am I patient with children's mishaps?
8. Do I listen to my children or just expect them to listen to me?
9. Do I allow others' opinions a fair hearing?
10. Am I cooperative with those with whom I live or work?
11. Do I see adversity as an obstacle to my happiness or as an opportunity to trust God?
12. Do I sacrifice integrity for a false veneer of looking good in front of others?

Third Temptation

Again, the devil took him to a very high mountain and showed him all the kingdoms of the world and their splendor; and he said to him, "All these I will give you, if you will fall down and worship me." Jesus said to him, "Away with you, Satan! for it is written, 'Worship the Lord your God, and serve only him'" (Matt 4:8-10).

1. Do I give God primacy in my life?
2. How much time do I give to God in prayer and study?
3. How much time do I give to God in service of others?
4. Do I assume my responsibility in my faith community?
5. Have I ever been violent in order to get order or control?
6. Do I deny the gospel in order to get ahead in business?
7. Is the safeguarding of my material possessions worth more than my brothers or sisters in need?
8. Do I worship my standard of living more than my God?
9. Am I consumed with ambition?
10. Have I ever kept silent when someone was being abused?
11. In what concrete way do I show that God is more important than anything else in my life?
12. Is consumerism an idol in my life?

Act of Sorrow

In your own words tell God you are sorry for any failings and sins that this prayer has brought to light. Thank God for the light of the Spirit. Rest peacefully in God's arms. Let the angels of God comfort you. God looks on you as blessed.

Chapter Three

A BEATITUDE PEOPLE

As disciples of Jesus we must learn from the master. So we travel to the mountainside with the people following Jesus, and we sit by his feet to listen. Jesus is going to teach us, to lead us from the old covenant into the new.

Moses met God on the mountain and descended alone with laws carved in stone. Jesus met God in the desert and returned to his people with the law of love enfleshed in his being. He gathered the people around him and poured out a passionate response to a loving God. The Beatitudes are the essence of the message of Christ. What the Commandments are to Moses, the Beatitudes are to Jesus. The Commandments are specific rules governing behavior. The Beatitudes are the compelling call of discipleship to the God of mercy.

The people surrounding Jesus are poor and oppressed; survival is a burden for most. Their hearts bear many sorrows; their expectations are few. By his words, Jesus simultaneously teaches and consoles. He carefully, compassionately leads his people to hope, based not on this world's satisfactions but on the living God.

Jesus looks upon his people and sees their suffering. Jesus looks on the woundedness of his people and reaches into their pain to draw out healing and comfort. Couching it in blessings, Jesus teaches the new law of mercy.

Poverty of spirit

"Blessed are the poor in spirit, for theirs is the kingdom of heaven" (Matt 5:3).

The spirit of poverty is knowing that God is all and we are not; the spirit of poverty is knowing that no human being can ever stand in judgment over another; the spirit of poverty is knowing that deference to others is an attribute of the kingdom of God. All this is blessed; all you who live in this way are blessed. No longer do you have to hold your head in shame because of apparent poverty of body or intellect or social standing. In the kingdom of God the lowest will be the highest; the least will be the greatest. A child will inherit what is denied the most powerful.

Jesus is calling his people to stand in their own blessings, to claim the truth of their beings. From all eternity they have been called into existence by a loving God; now all ages will call them blessed. Jesus is beginning the message that will only be completed when he is lifted on the cross at Calvary. The message is that powerlessness is the only power of the kingdom.

How difficult to understand the paradox and to embrace the reality. The marginalized, the mentally ill, the illegal aliens, the refugees, the homeless, and the abandoned young stand in readiness for the kingdom that is being denied the self-satisfied wealthy, the politically powerful, and the socially correct. Those who desire nothing but God possess all things in God and have no needs outside of God.

There is great mystery here that must be embraced before it can be understood. Deprivation of the most fundamental of human needs is not a detriment to attaining the kingdom of heaven; in fact, it can be an asset when combined with a surrendered heart. Jesus is not hoping that his people will be deprived of human needs and rights, but he is saying that nothing is an obstacle to happiness in God. Jesus is trying to teach his people not to cling to their possessions, their ideas, their plans, because none of these things fulfills their deepest desires. Love alone satisfies.

Sorrow

"Blessed are those who mourn, for they will be comforted" (Matt 5:4).

The promises of the kingdom continue—not only in eternal life, but here and now. When human efforts fail to comfort, God will touch the pain and in that touch console.

People sometimes limit the human experience to the predictable effects of environment and background. God refuses to be so constrained. If a child suffers terrible sexual and physical abuse there are many who say that the fullness of love and life are not possible because of the damaged psyche. Jesus tells us differently. Perhaps the child's ability to express love will not be measurable according to familiar standards, but nothing can harm that child permanently except personal free choices. No action of any other person, no matter how emotionally or psychologically devastating, can take anyone from the arms of God.

This concept is crucial to understanding the freedom from sorrow that Jesus promises. All the evil that is possible in the world is not greater than God's love. All the tragedy in the world is not greater than the mystery of God's healing touch. Again we cannot understand this; we simply allow the comfort of Jesus to break down the barriers of pain. We will feel the pain but we will not be alone in it, and we will not be destroyed by it. We will be comforted; our dry bones will return to life.

Resentment, bitterness and despair must be deliberately set aside. None of the Beatitudes can be passively accepted; they require decisions and commitments to the ways of God. They demand a surrender of control to God and to God alone. Sin and all its effects will have no control over a heart that has given all control to God. To be comforted by Jesus

is to make a conscious act of faith and trust in the limitless-
ness of God's love.

Responsibility accompanies every gift. As we are comforted so also do we comfort. The sorrows of others become
our own. We mourn the death of our enemy as we would
mourn the death of our own child. There are no victory pa-
rades after war or rallying cries for the execution of a murderer; we cannot rejoice in the defeat of anyone. There is
only sorrow for every person who suffers.

Forgiveness must be lived daily if we are to comfort those
in sorrow. Those who hurt us injure their own souls even
more. Bitterness and revenge eat away our happiness. For
our own well-being as well as for love of others, we have to
learn to forgive, to release others from the tombs of weakness
to which we have consigned them. Our forgiveness of others
is comfort for them when they suffer the pain of their own
weaknesses. And through the great mystery of love, forgiveness of others brings consolation to ourselves as well.

Meekness

"Blessed are the meek, for they will inherit the earth"
(Matt 5:5).

Each beatitude is not a separate reality; it is part of the essential message of unconditional love of God and others. The
Sermon on the Mount has always been accepted as the semi-
nal teaching of Jesus. The Beatitudes express fully the kingdom way. It is as if each beatitude nuances the love Jesus
embodies. To try to enter into an embrace of this love we
must glean understanding from each beatitude as we allow
the totality of all of them to pour over us.

In this beatitude, Jesus risks being called weak. After all,
anyone who refuses to fight back against injustices and personal wrongs must be a coward. Retaliation is a matter of
honor. Only wimps don't defend themselves, their families, or
their countries. The only language violent aggressors under-

stand is the language of superior force. The earth belongs to those with the greatest military might.

Jesus says "no." He destroys the myth that equates non-retaliation with inactivity, nonviolence with passivity. Jesus is clear: "turn the other cheek, walk the extra mile, love your enemy." Jesus doesn't just dismiss aggressive and domineering behavior; he encourages us to be conciliating and loving toward all. This is not passivity at all; it is determined active love. Strength, courage, and confidence are necessary for a person to develop meekness. It takes more heroism to stand before your enemy with a vulnerable heart than with an assault rifle or Patriot missile. In this beatitude, Jesus promises that those who remain open to their enemy will inherit the earth.

This goes contrary to the individualistic trend of looking out for Number One or of being on top of the corporate ladder. We don't expect to inherit anything; we try to seize what we want by skill or force. We admire and reward those who operate in this way, and we look down on those who don't have much ambition for advancement and prestige.

In business, allowing the needs of employees to come before corporate profits is not always encouraged or accepted. In family life, tolerance and acceptance of each member is often not the norm. In our recreational sports and games, fierce competitiveness rules. We live in a society that accepts corporate takeovers, looks the other way at spousal and child abuse, and supports violence in entertainment.

Meekness cannot be confused with failure to speak against abuses in the home or workplace or sports arenas. In the face of any threat or intimidation, the meek speak the truth fearlessly. And what they inherit is their own souls. Such people cannot be compromised. They are at peace with themselves and are able to receive the gifts of life without grabbing, hoarding or comparing. Meekness keeps us centered on God, at home with ourselves, and at peace with our brothers and sisters. Our inheritance is great!

Hunger for justice

"Blessed are those who hunger and thirst for righteousness, for they will be filled" (Matt 5:6).

We are hungry with a hunger that keeps us from being silent. We are hungry for bread withheld, for rights denied, for promises broken. We are hungry for compassion and mercy. We have been starved by capitalism and communism. Our throats are parched from militarism and materialism. We are so hungry, God.

We are guilty of social racism and economic segregation. The plight of the refugee is not our concern. We are morally hungry. Eager to assuage our hunger for justice, we forage for the food of prophecy. Where are our prophets to satisfy us? They are here; but even as we long for them, we routinely silence or ignore them when they appear before us. Their prescriptions for justice aren't convenient. They warn us against crying for justice for ourselves while oppressing others.

The prophets try to keep before us the pain of others, but we refuse to look. The problems of the homeless never go away. What is the point of expending energy on them? Why should we care for gay men with AIDS, since it's their own fault they contracted the disease? Drug addicts and criminals ought to be locked up forever because of their crimes. How easily attitudes of condemnation slip into our sense of justice.

Perhaps this is because we tend to look at justice from the viewpoint of a legal system that links justice with the apportioning of punishment. But the justice of the beatitudes has no room for the distribution of punishment. It is justice seasoned with mercy.

> And earthly power doth then show itself likest God's
> When mercy seasons justice . . .
> Though justice be thy plea, consider this,
> That in the course of justice, none of us
> Should see salvation. We do pray for mercy.

And that same prayer doth teach us all to render
The deeds of mercy.

(The Merchant of Venice, Act IV, Scene 1)

Through his prophets and by his own power of example, Jesus leads us from justice to mercy. The story of the Prodigal Son teaches mercy over justice. When the laborers in the vineyard received a day's pay for an hour's work, justice couldn't explain it. To forgive a brother or a sister seventy times seven times is not an example of justice. Some would say it is foolishness; Jesus would say it is love. Where justice would have demanded retribution or punishment, Jesus died asking forgiveness for his executioners. To be a disciple of Jesus we are, called to act justly, but we are called further than that; we are called to love tenderly, compassionately and mercifully.

Our hunger can be satisfied. Jesus continually and consistently offers us the food of righteousness, but on his terms. Those are the terms of love expressed in deeds of mercy. When we care about our brother's hunger we will be fed; when our sister's thirst is sated we will be refreshed ourselves. Our own hunger for justice leads us—like Jesus and with Jesus—to mercy.

Mercy

"Blessed are the merciful, for they will receive mercy" (Matt 5:7).

God doesn't put conditions on the graces we are given, but Jesus knows that we won't recognize or accept the gifts unless our hearts are open to them. Being merciful to others opens us to accepting the mercy of God for ourselves.

So many of us never accept forgiveness for past sins or weaknesses. We think our failings are unforgivable. God's mercy is refused through a false sense of unworthiness. Of course we are unworthy of God's forgiving love, but that has nothing to do with mercy. God chooses to love us and to forgive us. We allow God to be God and we accept being loved for no other reason than love itself.

In our human loves it is the same. We offend even those with whom we are intimate; we are offended by those with whom we are intimate. There is a need for the offer of forgiveness, but once given it becomes unimportant. The passion of renewed love wipes out any remnant of past offense.

> O happy fault, O necessary sin of Adam,
> which gained for us so great a Redeemer!
>
> Night truly blessed
> when heaven is wedded to earth
> and we are reconciled with God.
>
> (Easter Vigil Exsultet)

Every act of forgiveness between people is a share in the reconciliation Jesus accomplished on Calvary. The mercy which he gave with his life can be realized only when we ourselves freely give it. Forgiveness and mercy operate within a cycle of giving and receiving. One feeds the other. Our acts of mercy call down the mercy of God on us and on our enemies.

When Auschwitz was liberated in 1945, the following prayer was found clutched in the hands of a fourteen-year-old boy who had just died:

> O Lord,
> remember not only the men and women of good will,
> but also those of evil will.
> And in remembering the suffering
> they have inflicted upon us;
> honor the fruits we have borne
> thanks to this suffering—
> our comradeship, our compassion, our humility,
> our courage, our generosity,
> the greatness of heart
> which has grown out of all of this;
> and when they come to the judgment,

let all the fruits that we have borne,
be their forgiveness.

(Anonymous: Auschwitz)

This prayer calls down the mercy of God on the perpe-
trators of one of this century's greatest evils. This child held
on to this prayer. Somewhere in his young tortured heart wisdom grew. In his love, God was present because mercy was
present. Only when all of us possess such wisdom will we be
freed from the bondage of revenge and retaliation. Jesus is
leading us to this moment of freedom, a moment that opens
our eyes to God.

Purity of heart

"Blessed are the pure in heart, for they will see God"
(Matt 5:8).

If mercy opens our eyes, then purity of heart focuses them on
the face of God. By the covenant God made with us, we are
called to see God. Like every other gift from God this call is
not intended only for eternal life. It is true we will see God
clearly in eternity, but we are meant to experience some of
that sight here and now. God does not hide from our gaze; it
is we who fail to see. By keeping our hearts centered on God,
we will begin to see God.

Does this mean that only those who spend twenty-four
hours a day in contemplation can achieve purity of heart? Of
course not. Jesus did not preach the Sermon on the Mount to
a group of hermits; he was speaking to ordinary people who
had to work hard just to survive. In the midst of the daily
struggles of life we can keep our hearts open to the touch of
God and our ears open to the word of God.

Anyone who is responsible for a two-year-old child at
home is always alert to the sounds of the child, especially when
the child is not in the same room. We can make a similar com-
parison with our attention to God. While in the midst of the

chores of everyday life we can also be alert to the slightest sign of God. It may come in quiet or it may come at a time of high activity. It may be a simple awareness of the presence of our loving, gentle God or it may be a nudge to perform an act of mercy. Purity of heart keeps us uncomplicated and uncompromised in our loyalties. Purity of heart keeps us from substituting personal plans for the will of God. It keeps us from dividing our allegiances between God and other things. God isn't one among many gods. God is the one true God. To see God in all things and all people is to experience purity of heart.

When embraced, this single-heartedness permeates our whole lives. Purity is not restricted to matters of sexuality. It involves our whole being which is far more than an attribute of sexual conduct.

When we abide in the presence of the one who loves us intimately we experience purity. When we live in such a way that we express this same love, we live purity. When we see the face of God in an abandoned teenager hanging on the corner, we see purely. When we refuse to add to the scandal that is spreading about a neighbor, we show respect for our body and our neighbor's. When we love our enemy, we allow God to purify our heart.

Keeping rules will never give us purity of heart; it's just not enough. Purity is a matter of love, freely and passionately given by God and enthusiastically received by us. Our reward for such love will be the face of God seen in every other face we encounter. When our hearts are pure we see God always, and this sight gives us integrity of being which brings peace within ourselves and our communities.

Peace

> "Blessed are the peacemakers, for they will be called children of God" (Matt 5:9).

Peacemaking is a skill of the heart not of the intellect. To understand what Jesus is saying to us in this beatitude we must keep in our hearts all the messages he has given us in the first six.

We come to the task and gift of peacemaking carrying poverty of spirit to disarm us, sorrow to open us to God's consolation, meekness to strengthen us, hunger for justice to enflame us, mercy to free us from revenge, and purity to focus us on God alone. Peacemaking involves all of these qualities of heart.

If we are honest, we admit our weaknesses in many of these attributes. Does being a peacemaker imply a heroism beyond the norm? Yes and no. Yes, peace can only be achieved in the presence of people open to conversion to these ways of God. No, the heroism is not a personal requirement. There is one peacemaker–Jesus Christ. He is the one who completely fulfills all the prerequisites for peace. He alone does it.

Our role as peacemakers is to share in Jesus' way of peace. We have many failures and sins, but they do not keep us from allowing Jesus to use us for his work of peace. The essence is that we continue to make efforts towards peace, not that we achieve it totally.

There are days when we respond in anger, verbally attacking a friend or family member. That is not the work of peace. We repent, we seek forgiveness, we offer forgiveness. Now we are in the work of peace.

We make a conscious choice not to tolerate violence in our homes, yet we continue to allow the physical and sexual violence of movies on our television screens. We are inconsistent, imperfect in our stride toward the nonviolent life, but we persevere and continue to make efforts in that direction.

We say we do not believe in war or military aggression, yet we support colleges that depend heavily on ROTC (Reserve Officers' Training Corps) money. We continue to pay the telephone and income tax which pay for the military. Just because we are unable to do everything, we cannot refuse to do something. Step by step we study and pray and learn how to respond. In time and with grace we will be brought to fidelity.

We say we love all people, but on a daily basis we rarely meet the dispossessed or marginalized. All our friends and associates are from the same class of people. We live and work apart from the poor. By our own segregation we continue their oppression. The journey to equality and mutuality with all is a long one. We dare to begin it and trust God to make us determined to complete it.

We value our children's future, but we endanger it by the wastefulness of our living style. Greed consumes our energies and our earth. In God, we can learn to loosen our grip on possessions and self-satisfaction and risk entering into a willing interdependence with all beings great and small.

We spoil our children with material things and deny them our time and concern. We bring them up satisfying all their material needs but depriving them of a vibrant faith. Perhaps the love of our children will move us to really care for them and bring conversion to family life.

Finally we can only make peace when we embrace our enemy as brother or sister. The usual response to such a notion is: "No way!" However, if Jesus Christ, the Son of God, has taught us by word and by example to love our enemy, then we must do it. We must be capable of it in God's grace. This is our greatest task as peacemaker, to love the unlovable and to kiss the unkissable. In this way we will be recognized as children of God. In this way peace will come to the earth. And we will be blessed to have had a part in it.

Persecution

> "Blessed are those who are persecuted for righteousness' sake, for theirs is the kingdom of heaven" (Matt 5:10).

How strange it is that people of peace can pose such a threat to others. Sometimes it is because peacemakers must bring truth to light. Those with something to hide fear exposure.

Other times it seems as if moral integrity threatens in its own right.

Whatever the cause, the persecution is there. It is easily recognizable in the murders of missionaries and Christians in Central America or Africa. Persecution, however, also occurs much closer to home. It is felt by those who try to bring drug treatment centers or group homes for teenagers to middle-class neighborhoods. We are sophisticated today. Occasionally there will be a cross-burning but usually we persecute through zoning laws and legal action. We can keep people in the courts for years with restraining orders against a shelter or soup kitchen. No one denies the need for such places, they just don't want them in their neighborhoods. After all, such institutions adversely affect property values.

When we exclude certain people from our neighborhood or when we sign the petition to block low-income housing, we are persecuting the body of Christ. We are crying with the mob, "Crucify him, crucify him!" We need to recognize the fear that is pitting us against our brothers and sisters and pray for the conversion that will release us from that fear.

When we break from the crowd to do good, we might be accused of being naive, of being manipulated by people who could be helping themselves. When we sacrifice higher income for other values, such as time with family or time to share with the poor, we might be considered lacking in judgment.

Something as simple as saying grace before a meal in a restaurant is a risk and can be misinterpreted. But none of these insults or rejections can touch us. As we grow in God's life, they won't even offend us. For the beatitudes promise freedom. When we live them we experience the freedom of the children of God who are not bound to possessions or neighborhood or country. We experience release from resentment and retaliation. We find ourselves open to give mercy and to receive mercy. Sorrow no longer crushes us totally. People in need move from being threats to our lifestyles to being brothers and sisters.

And when we are the ones who face the hostile crowd for the sake of justice, we cling in faith to a God who feared nothing and returned love for hate, good for evil. We cannot stop people from persecuting us, but we can stop them from controlling us through fear or intimidation. We can choose our response to persecution. We have no need to be defensive; we have no need to protect ourselves. We are called to love and we will inherit the kingdom promised us.

The Beatitude Prayer of a Beatitude Person

Blessed are the poor in spirit, for theirs is the kingdom of heaven.
Blessed are those who mourn, for they will be comforted.
Blessed are the meek, for they will inherit the earth.
Blessed are those who hunger and thirst for righteousness, for they will be filled.
Blessed are the merciful, for they will receive mercy.
Blessed are the pure in heart, for they will see God.
Blessed are the peacemakers, for they will be called children of God.
Blessed are those who are persecuted for righteousness' sake, for theirs is the kingdom of heaven (Matt 5:3-10).

1. If possible, spend this prayer time outdoors. (If not, imagine yourself seated on a hillside.) Sit comfortably among the beauty of God's creation.
2. Acknowledge the presence of Jesus and listen as he speaks his beatitudes to you.
3. Also acknowledge that you are not alone. Many others are seated with you listening to Jesus.
4. Read the beatitudes over slowly a few times, letting them pour into you as healing balm for your spirit.
5. Ask Jesus to speak one beatitude to you in a unique way.

6. When you hear which beatitude Jesus is offering you, receive it as a precious gift.
7. Open your hands on your lap to receive the beatitude.
8. Place your hands over your heart and reverence the beatitude which you have received.
9. Pray for the grace to understand and appreciate this beatitude.
10. Listen to hear the call of Christ within it.
11. Spend time just reflecting on this grace.
12. When you are ready to get up, walk a few moments, aware that you are the embodiment of a beatitude of Jesus Christ. Let gratitude speak.

Chapter Four

NO ENEMIES ALLOWED

Even the Beatitudes with all their challenge cannot prepare us for the shock of Jesus' next words:

"You have heard that it was said, 'You shall love your neighbor and hate your enemy.' But I say to you, Love your enemies, and pray for those who persecute you, so that you may be children of your Father in heaven; for he makes his sun rise on the evil and on the good, and sends rain on the righteous and the unrighteous. For if you love those who love you, what reward do you have? Do not even the tax collectors do the same? And if you greet only your brothers and sisters, what more are you doing than others? Do not even the Gentiles do the same?" (Matt 5:43-47).

Jesus is clear; there is no doubt about what he means by his directive to love our enemy. Jesus intends us to love all people regardless of any action, race, creed, or nationality. The issue, then, is not "What did Jesus say?" but "How can we possibly live out this command?"

We can live it if we allow ourselves to fall in love with Jesus Christ. It is that simple and that drastic. Love of enemies can only be considered from a position of intimacy with Jesus—teacher, savior, priest, lover.

Nothing in the gospel revelation of the good news of the kingdom makes sense apart from the person of Jesus. Intellectual and literary analysis is insufficient for a reading of the gospel that leads to conversion. We must be with Jesus to understand the challenging words of Jesus. Relationship with Jesus is the fulcrum upon which everything else turns. It is Jesus, not some abstract doctrine, that is the cornerstone of our faith. It is Jesus who lives in us, who interprets the gospel in our everyday life.

We strive to love our enemies because Jesus tells us to. That is sufficient motive. With Jesus we dare to risk the impossible. The presence of Jesus gives us the conviction that all things are possible, even love of enemies.

In Jesus, there actually are no enemies. Jesus changed all relationships once he became one of us. No longer do family blood lines alone determine brother and sister. No longer do we categorize anyone as friend or foe, family or stranger. Everyone is simply a child of God and, as such, a brother or sister to each of us.

Since Christ shed his blood on Calvary we are bound to each other. The stranger no longer exists in a Christic sense. National boundaries become meaningless when God is Father and Mother to everyone. The face of our enemy bears the trace of divine lineage. No one can be dismissed as unimportant, disposable, or beyond redemption; no one is outside the love offered by a God who lets "the sun rise on the good and bad."

All of Jesus' teaching and example call for a total conversion to the ways of God from the ways of society. Sometimes attempts to make religion adaptable to our needs has clouded the clarity of the call. The gospel reaches into every aspect of our daily lives: business, social, political, family. Religion is not one slice of life among many. If lived the way Christ intended it, religion is all of life. And love of enemies is a determining factor in the religion taught by Jesus Christ.

Love of enemies is the mark of the Christian that cannot be ignored as irrelevant, glossed over as unimportant or abandoned as unattainable. More often than not we Christians do choose to ignore or dismiss this imperative. We consider it an option for those few extremists who refuse to hate or retaliate against evil with force. That is, we allow love of enemies for some but we don't expect it of all. Perhaps it is time for a thorough reconsideration of love of enemies with the hope that it will lead to an honest attempt to live it as well as understand it.

How to love our enemies: Pray and make choices

If we want to learn how to love our enemies, the starting point is to believe that it is the desire of Jesus that we do so. Acting out of this belief, we pray for the grace to love our enemy. Such love is the work of God, so we must be in the presence of God to attempt it.

Putting aside all preconceived ideas which have been culturally embedded in us over centuries, we try to honestly admit what love of enemies excludes and what it involves. Since we cannot love and hate simultaneously, love of enemies excludes hatred of anyone for any reason, no matter how justified we might think it. This surrender of hatred is not a matter of feeling; it is choice. To control feelings of hatred in our lives we consciously try to stop all expressions of hatred. We try to cease spending any time, effort, or expense on hatred.

To take a common example: someone has hurt us by belittling us in front of others. We have witnesses; we know what the person said about us. Whether or not it was true, it felt cruel and humiliating. Feelings of anger lead to feelings of hatred. What does love of enemy mean in this situation? It means we actively work against our feelings, which is hard work. We do not return insult for insult. Nor do we spread gossip about the person who wounded our reputation. Instead, we pray for the person. If truth has been denied, we may have to speak the truth but only to those for whom it is necessary. We calmly dismiss thoughts of retaliation and plans for revenge as temptations against charity. We do not try to discredit our opponent's reputation as a way of defending ourselves. We continue to show respect and concern for this person in all future relations.

Actions such as these lead to a pattern of tolerance and forgiveness in our relations with others. As seen in this one example, there is nothing passive about love of enemy. Resistance to revenge demands positive actions to turn from the path of enmity. To endure evil with love, which is what love of enemies is, is the most active work in which a person can engage. Self-control and respect for our accuser are far more difficult than senseless rage and violent retaliation.

Watch how others love their enemies.

A great deal of what we learn in life comes through the example of other people. Football players watch games over and over to grasp techniques that might be helpful. Children mimic everything they see and learn to act through observing others; adolescents spend hours watching the same performer so they can dance the same steps. We watch craft demonstrations and cooking shows to learn a new skill. In the same way, it is possible to learn love of enemies by observing others doing it.

A woman who has been faithfully married for many years faces a spouse who announces he is leaving her for someone else. She is stunned. There is no question of reconciliation; he wants out of the marriage and moves in with the new lover. Divorce proceedings begin. Unspeakable pain, rejection, and anger seem to overwhelm all other feelings in the woman. Yet she deliberately chooses to pray every day for her husband, in spite of all the feelings of hatred that are coursing through her body. She speaks the truth, acknowledges her feelings, but continues to show concrete expressions of respect for him. The divorce process takes time and communication. She sets limits but she does not seek revenge. Many months pass before healing even seems within sight. Some wounds might remain open all her life, but the active love expressed will bring the healing power of God into this and every situation of pain. Healing is the fruit of love of enemy.

A teacher in a school for disturbed children is attacked by two adolescents. They go for his eyes. He tries to protect himself; he calls for help but he does not physically assault the boys. Other teachers come and restrain the students, using methods that will not hurt the boys in any way. Immediately after the incident, the teacher is sitting catching his breath and assessing the damage to his eyes. The teacher is young, athletically active, and physically strong—a weight lifter. His first comments are concern for the students involved. He knows they will be as upset by the violence as he is. He cries and explains, "I am not crying because I am hurt but because of the tension I am feeling from not hitting the boys. I never realized how much strength it takes to show restraint; it would have been easier to hit the boys than not to." Restraint was an active experience, not a passive one.

Practice love of enemies.

This is not an attempt to give even a sample of stories about people who have loved their enemies in ordinary life. These few examples are given to jostle our imaginations to find creative ways of responding to evil with love. There isn't a manual for loving our enemies. In fact, for many of us, the examples that we have seen in our own lives are few. On a social level, we are in the infancy stage in learning alternatives to violence and revenge. We learn to walk by walking, to talk by talking. We learn to love our enemies by acting with love toward them.

Recognizing our traditions of violence and our refusal to believe in the Sermon on the Mount, we still begin in our time and in our place to love our enemies. It will be trial and error. In the process we will be converted and we will learn.

Approach the enemy with openness.

Once we decide to love our enemies we have to meet them. We have to see their faces and hear their voices. Society usually keeps us at a distance from our enemy. We avoid living in the neighborhoods of those who are different. In war we bomb targets, not individuals, and we refer to civilian deaths as "collateral damage." For those supporting abortion, a fetus is considered an inconvenience, not an unborn child. In our justice system, state-condoned murder is called capital punishment. Death-row inmates are labeled as animals; we don't want to hear of their pain or their backgrounds. We want to eliminate them instead of meeting them.

Slogans and causes keep us from seeing and hearing the human face of our enemy. Before we commit ourselves to any action against our enemy we must learn to listen with our hearts as well as with our ears, and we must listen as Jesus. We look in the faces of our enemies and we allow ourselves to see their pain. We listen to the cries of our enemies and we allow ourselves to hear their torment. In faith we believe that our enemy can shed light on what is true. We are in pursuit of truth, the reflection of God. Even the tyrant dictator has a piece of the truth. The convicted murderer has a piece of the truth, and the crabby, arrogant neighbor who opposes us on every issue has a piece of the truth.

Listening is easy when we are trying to get material to defend our own position; it is difficult when we are trying to understand. Listening for the purpose of loving is intense and prayerful. We know it is beyond us, but we trust in God's desire that we love and we try. And we must try to continue to love even when we think there is nothing left to love.

A poignant story of loving through hard times is portrayed in the play, *A Raisin in the Sun*. It shows a ghetto family dealing with one of their own who has made a foolish mistake of judgment thus losing their entire savings. The savings were intended to be down-payment for a house of their own away from the slums. The mother of the family keeps the perspective clear and the love focused as she refuses to allow the young man to be abandoned by his sister.

> There is always something left to love. And if you ain't learned that, you ain't learned nothing. Have you cried for that boy today? I don't mean for yourself and for the family . . . I mean for him: what he been through and what it done to him. Child, when do you think is the time to love somebody the most? When they done good and made things easy for everybody? Well then, you ain't through learning—because that ain't the time at all. It's when he's at his lowest and can't believe in hisself 'cause the world done whipped him so! When you starts measuring somebody, measure him right, child, measure him right. Make sure you done taken into account what hills and valleys he come through before he got to wherever he is.[3]

Speak words of love.

There will be times when we will know the valleys that our enemy has traveled, and that may make it easier to love. But there will be many times when we will have to love blindly. Only after the act of love will knowledge come. There is a story told of St. Francis of Assisi and a leper he met on the road. The sight of the leper sickened Francis and he couldn't bear the thought of touching him. Francis fought down the instinct to run and kissed the leper. The kiss broke the fear and Francis was freed of any disgust he had originally experienced. The point is that Francis overcame his revulsion of the leper only after he kissed him.

After we have listened to our enemy, the next step is to speak in kindness and compassion. Francis' kiss was an unspoken word of love. Spoken or unspoken is immaterial as long as the message of love and respect is conveyed to our enemy. Of course, this effort does not guarantee that our enemy will respond in the same way. That part is not our concern. Regardless of the response, our words must be words of love and our expressions must be expressions of love.

Lest there be misunderstanding here about participating in or condoning evil acts, it is important to distinguish between the action and the person of our enemy. Acceptance of a person does not imply acceptance of that person's behavior. We can make this distinction, and we need to make it often. At the same time that we listen to and show respect for our enemy we can also actively work against any actions which we think are not in accord with the principles of Christ.

For example, a person who abuses children cannot be allowed to continue in that pattern. If we know about it, we must act to make the abuse public in order to stop it and to clarify reality for the child. The child needs to know that what was done was wrong and unacceptable and not any fault on the child's part. Secrecy gives mixed messages to the hurt child. Open discussion is important for healing and for prevention of further abuse. We make no concessions that will endanger the child. Yet, at the same time, we treat with compassion the perpetrator and try to get services for that person as well as for the child.

Another contemporary situation that calls for clarity is the position of anti-abortion activists and pro-abortion supporters. There is no doubt that abortion is contrary to the message of Jesus. The fetus may seem like an enemy to the woman carrying him or her, but Jesus tells us to love our enemies, so the pregnant woman must love that fetus and do what is best for the unborn child. However, under no circumstances can anyone presume to judge the persons who are contemplating abortions or even those who perform them. We resist the practice of abortion but we love the abortionists. The words we speak to them cannot be words of violence, hatred, or condemnation; they can only be words of love. Some pro-life people do not speak with respect or compassion to pro-choice opponents. Not only does Jesus insist that we love the fetus but that we love the one who is trying to terminate the fetus.

To speak with love implies that silence is insufficient in the face of evil or injustice. Indeed, silence in such circumstances implies complicity. To speak with love calls for courage. If others are zoning out lower income people from our neighborhood, love of enemies requires us to speak against the zoning laws, thus risking the hatred of our neighbors. If there is slander, gossip, or degrading speech at our workplace, to remain silent is to consent to it. We cannot control how people talk, but we can refuse to participate in it. We can walk away and make known why we are doing so.

We are called to speak against racism, sexism, militarism, and any behavior which is contrary to the teachings and example of Jesus. This is active love of enemy, and it is desperately needed in today's society. The follower of Christ is the one who speaks these words and, when necessary, follows words of truth with actions for justice.

Acknowledge hatred.

Part of the work of loving our enemies is to ask forgiveness from God and from each other for sins against love. All Christians can pray for forgiveness. Catholics can do this in a sacrament. Again, feelings don't count here. We may still feel hatred; but if we are sorry and want to work against letting hatred control our behavior, we can profit by confessing our weakness. God will not be silent to our plea for a pure heart. In time, if we don't put up obstacles, we will receive it.

The Sacrament of Reconciliation is a concrete way of deliberately disarming our heart and emotions. It is a step toward the other in peace; it allows God the opening to transform our hearts of stone into hearts of flesh. In our own healing the world will also experience healing. As we acknowledge our need for forgiveness, we can be led to be more tolerant of others and to practice forgiveness.

Practice love daily.

Finally, love of enemies becomes a part of everyday life as it becomes lived. As we need to eat and sleep every day, so also we need to pray and practice love of enemies every day. It is not something we learn once and for all. We pray daily for the insight and grace to know what step to take toward our enemy. Then, in God's presence and with God's grace, we take that first step. It leads us to our next insight; the process is unending: we go from praying for the insight to making the step which leads to the next inspiration and the next step. Gandhi called this process the "experiment in truth."

Catholics can also learn to love their enemies through participation in Eucharist, by their active presence at the greatest act of nonviolent love the world has ever seen. Jesus gives his life to those who reject him and we are with him in this most sacred act. To enter into Eucharist to be transformed is to allow Jesus to take us and use us for the salvation of the world. Daily Eucharist, when accompanied by self-surrender and abandonment to the will of God, leads us to the daily practice of living and loving as Jesus does—which includes love of enemies.

In this time of earthly pilgrimage none of us will ever arrive at perfect love of enemy. No two of us will be at the same place along the journey to perfect love. It is of no consequence. What matters is not where each of us is, but that we are all moving along the way. Disciples of Christ are those people who keep on trying and who refuse to give up on the ways of Christ because of personal weaknesses or failures. We strive to make love of enemies an abiding effort in us. We presume it is never an accomplished reality.

Love of Enemies

"You have heard that it was said, 'You shall love your neighbor and hate your enemy.' But I say to you, Love your enemies and pray for those who persecute you" (Matt 5:43-44).

This is intended to be a prayer of petition for yourself and for the world.

1. Find a crucifix and hold it in your hands during this prayer time.
2. Read the scripture passage at the top of the page.
3. Look at the crucifix and read the passage again, focusing on Christ's commitment to unconditional love.
4. Begin to pray by name for all those persons who have hurt you in any way. After each name, pray: "Lord, forgive them," and kiss the crucifix.
5. Pray by name for any persons who consider you their enemy. After each name, pray: "Lord, have mercy," and kiss the crucifix.
6. Name some situations of enmity anywhere in your milieu or in the world. After each one, pray: "Lord, teach us to love," and kiss the crucifix.
7. Simply look at the crucifix and say, "Thank you."
8. Place the crucifix in your car or in your bedroom to remind you to pray for your enemies.

Chapter Five

SACRAMENT OF PASSION

One day during a workshop on peace and nonviolence a man who claimed to be an atheist was speaking of love for enemies. He was a committed, concerned person who had spent years helping the homeless in New York City. He said that he didn't think it was possible to love our enemies unless we believe in God. His own experience was that, without God, as far as he could get was not to harm his enemies. He could not make the leap into love.

This may be only one man's experience, but I think it a profound and valid commentary on a most difficult task. As a Christian and a Catholic my own experience is similar to this man's. I cannot love my enemies without a close union with God. To be more specific, I find that I cannot continue the effort to respond to evil with love and to see as brother or sister the one who is harming me without the help of daily union with Jesus Christ in Eucharist.

Love of enemies is the message of Christ, and we need the person of Christ to live it. Jesus Christ is present to us intimately by our Baptism and is present to us in our union of love with one another. But there is no greater intimacy than the union offered us in Eucharist—the moment of Jesus' perfect love of enemies and reconciliation of the whole world with God.

Mohandas Gandhi, a Hindu ascetic, recognized Jesus' death as the perfect act of love it was: "a man [Jesus] who was completely innocent, offered himself as a sacrifice for the good of others, including his enemies, and became the ransom of the world. It was a perfect act."[4] We know that we share in this act every time we participate in Eucharist.

Eucharist is our moment to touch God. We are people of flesh and blood, not merely abstract spirits. We need to touch. There are times when, like the apostle Thomas after the Resurrection, we need to put our hands into the side of Christ—not only to restore our faith but to nourish our hearts.

> But Thomas (who was called the Twin), one of the Twelve, was not with them when Jesus came. So the other disciples told him, "We have seen the Lord." But he said to them, "Unless I see the mark of the nails in his hands, and put my finger in the mark of the nails and my hand in his side, I will not believe."

> A week later his disciples were again in the house, and Thomas was with them. Although the doors were shut, Jesus came and stood among them and said, "Peace be with you." Then he said to Thomas, "Put your finger here and see my hands. Reach out your hand and put it in my side. Do not doubt but believe" (John 20:24-27).

We reach out, we grasp, we hold, we pour out our perfume, we caress, and we are formed by the One to whom we cling. If we touch the face of Christ, we see as Christ sees. If we lean on Christ's heart, we move to its rhythm. If we hold the hand of Christ, we do his work. If we put our feet next to Christ's, we go where he goes.

Just as compelling as our physical need for Christ—no, infinitely more compelling—is his desire for us. It's easy to understand our need for Christ, but can we ever comprehend Christ's longing for us? Can we live with the consequences of being so lovable?

Awareness of Christ's love pursues us relentlessly until we respond. However blindly at first, we stretch out our hands and hearts toward the source of love. Our entire beings become sensitive to the awesome presence of God. Leaving behind all that would hinder us from following freely, we run toward God.

Touching Christ

How can we gain access to the infinite God of mountains and majesty? Is it not beyond us? Is it only in our imagination and desires that we touch God? Can we experience the physical reality that Thomas experienced in the upper room? God does not change. Jesus as God does not change. He will not deny us the physical touch that he freely allowed Thomas. He will not deny us his physical body—not only to gaze upon, but to embrace. Such union with Christ is not reserved for mystics or exceptionally holy men and women. Every baptized Christian is called to the same intimate union and physical contact with Christ. When we feed the hungry and give drink to the thirsty, we touch Christ. When we console the sorrowing selflessly and bear wrongs patiently, we touch Christ. And when we enter into the offering of Christ to his Father for us on Calvary, we touch Christ.

Intimate union with Christ is offered us in the Eucharist. The one perfect act in which all the fire, passion, revelation, majesty, power, vulnerability, and glory of God is expressed in its totality is the offering of Jesus to His Father on Calvary, celebrated by us in the Holy Sacrifice of the Mass.

The Mass is not just a reminder of Calvary or a symbolic reenactment of the death of Christ. When we are present at the Sacred Liturgy, we actually become present to the death of Jesus Christ. There is no explaining this mystery. It is an act of love on God's part to invite us to the banquet and an act of faith on our part to believe.

To be with Jesus at his moment of perfect love for us is the most intimate act we can experience as human beings. We may not feel emotionally aroused. In fact, we may feel cold and indifferent. But intimacy does not rest on our feelings; union does not depend upon warm thoughts. The power of love is beyond the limits of our emotions. Union with Christ at Mass is more powerful and fulfilling and passionate than any physical union between persons.

Calvary is the climax of Jesus' abandonment in love, and we are invited to be with him at that moment. "I do not call you servants any longer, because the servant does not know what the master is doing; but I have called you friends, because I have made known to you everything I have heard from my Father" (John 15:15). What Jesus knows of the Father is not mere intellectual knowledge. It is knowing in the biblical sense of being physically one with the Father. And that intimacy Jesus is offering to us. We will receive into our bodies at Communion the physical Body and Blood of Jesus, the Incarnate Word of God. It is consummated.

Opportunity for passionate love

Consummation is the key to surrendering to Eucharist and to being transformed by it. There is no question here of ever understanding Eucharist. It is mystery, and mysteries are not grasped or understood; they are reverenced and embraced. Eucharist is not an abstract doctrine requiring our assent. Eucharist is Jesus Christ's passionate abandonment to his Father in which we are invited to share. The sharing is at the level of consummation.

We are entering into the language of love to speak of an act of love. God is intimately one with Jesus Christ and, through the Spirit, desires to bring us into that same intimacy. No human love can measure itself against the passion of God's love. We are called by our Baptism to enter into Christ's passion; Eucharist is the experience of this passion.

Emotional feelings are not the issue here—truth is. The truth is that Jesus Christ surrendered in his full humanity and equally full divinity to the embrace of his Father at the cost of his human life. It was real flesh and blood, pain and suffering that was surrendered on Calvary. All human passion expressed in the physical surrender of the body takes its value from this great act of intimacy. Whether married, single, celibate, religious, or lay, we are called in Eucharist to the passionate surrender of our bodies to Christ.

To share in Eucharist fully we dare surrender and risk passion. We long for love; we need to be filled. Daily we come to the table to eat the Bread of Life because daily we need the food of God to nourish our spirits and enflame our passion. Sometimes people live lives without passion; sometimes people participate in Eucharist without passion. Both experiences are devoid of the fullness for which we are created.

Eucharist is love and, as love, it cannot be experienced in total passivity. No matter how inspiring the homily or beautiful the liturgy, the fruits of Eucharist cannot be received if it is merely attended. On the other hand, no matter how poor the homily, derelict the priest, or shabby the liturgy, nothing can limit our experience of Eucharist if it is an act of passionate surrender. Eucharist cannot be measured by human standards nor bound by human limitations. Christ is in loving union with the Father; we are in loving union with Christ and the Father.

In Eucharist we have the opportunity to respond day after day with desire and commitment. Despite our feelings, we desire union and choose surrender. Beyond our fears we allow Christ to draw us into abandonment. "I remained, lost in oblivion; My face reclined on the Beloved. All ceased and I abandoned myself, Leaving my cares forgotten among the lilies."[5]

An experience of death

As we reflect on the act of Jesus offering himself to the Father, we must not gloss over the reality of the human suffering in it. Jesus Christ was tortured and executed; he suffered every painful detail of that in his mind and body. His friends and relatives suffered with him. The promise of redemption did not alleviate the real suffering of crucifixion.

Eucharist is the memorial of the Lord's death, and we celebrate in the joy of resurrection. However, we must pause to acknowledge the dark moments before resurrection. We do this, not out of a sense of morbidity or guilt; neither of these contribute anything to holiness. We do this rather to see clearly what is involved in Eucharist.

Jesus Christ was rejected and condemned to death because of his fidelity to the will of God. During Jesus' experience of temptation in the desert, he chose to be faithful to the ways of God, to renounce all alliance with power and to allow no other force in his life except the force of love. As he went about preaching in Galilee, Jesus taught his people the same message of compassion and mercy.

By his associations with all the powerless, marginalized people of his day—lepers, tax collectors, prostitutes, Samaritans, the blind and lame, the possessed and disturbed—Jesus modeled the behavior of God. For all of this, for his life and message, Jesus was hunted down and tried as a criminal. He upset the politically and spiritually powerful by refusing to have anything to do with power. He upset the state by not giving it any authority over the children of God. Jesus rendered the state powerless by not bending to its illusion of power.

Such fidelity costs. For Jesus the price was death. Eucharist remembers this death and makes us present to this great act of redemptive love. Eucharist calls us to do the same—to make decisions to live the way of God, to show the fruit of those decisions by works of mercy, and to be willing to stand for God even at the expense of personal suffering. Willingness to suffer even unto death is crucial to Eucharist.

If this is starting to sound impossible, then we are approaching the truth of Eucharist. Such love is impossible except for God; and we are called to this love. We approach Eucharist because God invites us and will strengthen us to live as people of God, which is always beyond the possible.

By its nature Christianity is a revolutionary way of life; and Eucharist, in its extreme of self-offering love, exemplifies the radical nature of Christian faith, hope, and love. Eucharist brings us to be a part of the suffering and death of Christ and therefore a part of the redemption from all suffering and death. Any pain we endure is part of the pain of Christ present at Eucharist.

In the presence of inconsolable grief in life, Eucharist does not give us words to explain the pain; but it gives us a person who mourns with us and promises us life in the face of death, hope in the face of despair, and joy in the face of misery.

Simply bread

Amazingly, all this wonder and mystery of life, death, resurrection, and redemption comes to us as everyday food. Jesus shares this most sacred act in the simplicity of a meal. We can ritualize it in grand cathedrals with clerics dressed in the robes of medieval nobility, cloud the altar in incense, and keep the congregation at a safe distance in the pews. But we can also ritualize it in a hut, with the congregation gathered around a piece of bread and a cup of wine.

All over the world, in every different language, we begin the celebration of Eucharist by laying down our burdens. Our sins are our burdens. "Lord have mercy. Christ, have mercy. Lord, have mercy." There is no need to carry our sins with us. We are in the presence of Christ who offers us release from sin and all its effects. With every cry for mercy we join all the people of God in leaving sin at Christ's feet.

We rise now. We rise to meet our God. We listen to the Word of God as proclaimed in the readings. They bring us into the living history of the people of God. We hear the stories of people who sinned and failed, who loved and sang, who fled God and seduced God. We hear the good and the bad. We hear the living gospel of Jesus' life on this earth, of how he struggled to follow the will of God, of how he danced with his people and cried with them. Reflection is shared on the gospel; sometimes it seems helpful, sometimes not. The eloquence of the preacher is not the measure of the impact of the Word of God in our hearts and lives.

Our minds have been opened by the scripture, our hearts stirred. Now we are ready to respond. Gifts brought to the altar from the rear of the Church signify the offering of ourselves that we all bring to the altar. As necessary as the ordained priest is, so also is the congregation. So necessary that the Second Vatican Council suggested that priests not offer Mass unless there is a congregation. Our presence as the people of God offering ourselves to be transformed is as crucial to Eucharist as is the priest's offering of the bread and wine.

Once offered, we are now on that altar with the bread and wine waiting for the transforming power of God to change us into the body and blood of Christ. Christ will not refuse our request. No matter how poor the offering, how sinful the offerer, he comes to us. No matter the weakness of our faith, he fans the slightest spark with his own response. "This is my body; this is my blood." We are all transformed over and over until that day when we see God face to face and receive total transformation in eternity with God.

Now that Christ's sacrifice is complete we dare to say "Our Father," the prayer of the children of God. On our own strength it is not possible to clasp hands as brothers and sisters. In God's presence it is the only thing possible. And we can do more than clasp hands; we can use these hands to bring peace to one another because we have been brought into the Body and Blood of Peace Incarnate. Peacemakers move from the intimacy of transformation by God into the acceptance of the potential intimacy of all people with God and one another.

Jesus comes to the table with us; he feeds us the bread of life, his Body. He holds out the cup of wine, his Blood, for us to drink freely. How simply Jesus expresses the greatest of all mysteries! He knows us so well. We need to eat every day; we need to be nourished and fed over and over. We get weary and weak and come to the table for refreshment and strength. We fail in our attempts to be loving and we need to be renewed by the source of all love. Our clothes may be tattered and our spirits frayed, but the bread of angels is ours.

A Eucharistic minister holds before us a small wafer of bread with the proclamation: "Body of Christ." Our "Amen" signals that we accept that we as well as the bread are now the Body and Blood of Christ. We consume the Lamb of God and surrender to being consumed by the Lamb of God. Amen to the willingness to be given in sacrifice for others. "This is my body, which is given for you. Do this in remembrance of me . . . This cup that is poured out for you is the new covenant in my blood" (Luke 22:19-20).

Through his name, in his name, and with his name, we eat and drink. And we are sent in peace for peace. We are God's now. All is God's now.

Eucharist

For this prayer you will need water—lots of it. Pray this prayer while swimming in a lake or an ocean or a swimming pool. Or make this prayer while soaking in a tub of hot water or standing under a pulsing shower. Wherever you are, make sure you are alone and can be relatively sure of a time of uninterrupted solitude.

1. When surrounded by water, hear the words of Christ: "This is my body; this is my blood."

2. Allow the totality of Christ's gift to you in Eucharist to surround you as completely as the water does.
3. Contemplate the fact that Eucharist is not a prayer we say but an immersion into the passionate surrender of Christ to his Father for love of us.
4. Just let the water be the medium of surrender for this prayer. As the water envelops you, let this great act of love envelop you also.
5. Feel the cleansing, refreshing water of life nurture your body.
6. Allow your own body to enter into the water of life and the passion of Christ.
7. When you emerge from your water source, notice that there is no part of you that is not wet, no part not touched by the water. There is no part of us individually or communally that is not influenced by Eucharist.
8. Love of Eucharist, commitment to it is the only appropriate response to this prayer.

Chapter Six

VESSELED VIRGIN

As we contemplate Christ offering himself to the Father and to us in Eucharist, we allow his words to penetrate our minds, hearts, and bodies. "This is my body, this is my blood." How can we—finite beings, limited humanity—hold the body and blood of God? Can we accept the seed of God and allow it to grow within us to nourish and heal our starving, broken world? Can we accept the call to be Christ?

Jesus, as God and man, could face the temptations of power, choose to act only out of love, resist all dependence upon force, love his enemies even to the point of giving his life for them. Jesus could be passionately surrendered and recklessly abandoned to his Father. On the strength of such love, Jesus could be the peace he promised. And he will be. But can we be peace to one another?

The amazing thing is that Jesus will be peace through us. Jesus has gone beyond the bestowal of love; he has brought us into relationship with him in the spread of this love. Jesus has shared divinity with us as well as humanity; and he has done so through the body of one who was like us in every way. Jesus began the work of redemption in the Spirit-penetrated womb of Mary.

If we are serious about being the body of Christ in our time, we need to be with Mary. She held the child Jesus in her arms and said, as no other human being could ever say, "This is my body, this is my blood." Called to the same vocation of Christ-bearer, we must learn from the one who did it first and most completely. If we wish to drink deeply of the transformed wine of peace, we must listen to the woman who advised us: "Do whatever he tells you."

In the mission of peace which is the mission of establishing the reign of God, Mary is vesseled virgin, faithful disciple, presiding priest, and Spirit-filled guide. To relate to Mary is to share in this mission. Zeal for the mission urges us to stay close to this most faithful missionary. As an ancient Arabic proverb says, "If you want fragrance, stay close to the seller of perfumes." We desire to be Christ, so we stay near the bearer of Christ.

Virgin of Israel

As we did with Christ, it helps in the beginning if we see Mary in her historical context. Mary was a young Hebrew woman steeped in the religious and cultural traditions of her people. She had parents, cousins, and neighbors. She was in relationship with those who were part of her everyday life. She had a man with whom she was in love, to whom she was betrothed. In most details her life was ordinary.

With her relatives and friends Mary would have gone to the temple to worship God and to pray for the deliverance of their people. Like all Israelites, she lived in anticipation of the Messiah. Mary was intimately bound to these people; and yet, from all eternity, she was set apart from them. Some close to her may have had a sense of the holiness of God expressing itself in Mary more clearly than in anyone else, but for most, the graces would have gone unnoticed. God's gifts to Mary were not to remove her from her people but to immerse her in the act of their redemption.

As a Hebrew girl, Mary would have been taught the history of her people; she would have learned of their sin and their grace. She would have learned their prayers and their cries for deliverance. The God of the covenant was Mary's God, the God of Abraham and Sarah, Moses and Myriam, David and Bathsheba. The God of the Israelites was always involved with the people, whether they were sinful or faithful. This God never gave up hope in them. But this God longed for a people who would turn with their whole heart and soul in worship and love. In Mary, the longing of God was fulfilled, and the longing of the people of God would be fulfilled in her son.

Mary was loved by God, and she loved God. She was chosen to bear the mark of God's love in a way that no other person ever had. She was prepared and readied to let the Spirit of God consummate her union with God so the Son of God could take flesh in her body.

When the time God had deemed appropriate came, a messenger was sent to this young girl of Galilee to ask for her consent. Even though Mary had surely surrendered herself to God many times and would have allowed God to use her without asking her permission, God gives Mary the opportunity to respond. We see in this question conveyed by an angel a sign of the respect God gives all of us.

God is our creator and freedom is part of our wondrous creation, so dearly are we valued and so highly trusted. And God gave Mary freedom. God sought Mary's consent. There was no pressure or force. God would wait on the loving response of a creature to fulfill the plan of the creator.

Mary questioned God's messenger; she had to be clear as to what she was being asked. The angel was direct: you will conceive a child by the power of God's spirit, and this child will be God's son. Mary understood. Consent filled her being. God became man.

This surrender reveals Mary in the purity of her response. The risk of a pregnancy outside marriage was not greater than the trust Mary had in her God. Mary knew God so well and loved God so passionately that she abandoned all thoughts of self-preservation and self-interest. God was trustworthy, so there was no fear in Mary's abandonment, no need for stoically heroic actions on her part, for decisions undertaken with gritted teeth and controlled will. Mary was utterly confident in the ways of God and completely in love with the being of God. Her leap of faith was into the arms of a God who loved her intimately, who caressed her constantly, and who pierced her heart with a sword.

In her act of abandonment and surrender, Mary became an open vessel for God. She became a being of pure receptivity at the disposal of God exclusively. She could then bear Christ. We receive the same call. We are drawn in love to surrender our choices; we are seduced by God to abandon our desires; and we will be opened by God to receive the seed of God.

We are called to give flesh to Jesus in our bodies. Jesus the man will not be born again in the same way he was born of Mary, but he will be born in a new way if we allow ourselves to be vesseled virgins as Mary was. We share vocation with the Mother of God, the vocation of bringing Christ into the world.

Disciple of Christ

To stop at motherhood as Mary's greatest moment would be to deny her the growth she experienced as she listened and watched her son develop; in particular, as she watched him preaching, teaching, and healing. Her years of forming and nurturing Jesus passed into the time of Jesus' forming and nurturing his Church. As Jesus moved into his adult ministry, Mary moved from mothering to missioning. We also move from being nurtured by God to being sent by God, from being brought into the Church by Baptism to being responsible for the Church through mission.

Jesus fed the multitude and healed many, but he also invited some to follow him more closely, to learn from him, to help him in his work. These were his disciples. Mary was among those who followed Jesus in his public ministry. She was mother but became disciple. We know from the gospel that she is with him on three separate occasions in his public life. Since Jesus never traveled very far from his home, it is a fair assumption that Mary was with him often. She heard the beatitudes, witnessed his acts of mercy, observed the reactions of people to him. She learned from the son she taught.

Mary pondered her son's message as she had pondered the message of Simeon many years earlier. Like Jesus, Mary sensed her son's rejection by his own people. Words of compassion, peace, forgiveness, and tolerance threaten the complacent and self-satisfied. Yet these same words came like a healing balm to a troubled people. Some recognized Jesus as their long-awaited savior. Mary witnessed both reactions to her son; she felt his pain and shared his hope.

Through all this Mary continued to learn from Jesus. Never before had God spoken so clearly. This was the time of redemption, the time of the coming of the reign of God. Even her own life of abandonment to the will of God couldn't have prepared Mary for the wonder of her son's life. God had always reached out to the poor and oppressed and shown them mercy, but now God was one of them in Jesus.

Jesus was with his people. He couldn't seem to get enough of them. Jesus related to the centurion and the Samaritan, called the tax collector, ate with sinners, and let a prostitute wash his feet. He sent a woman, known for her sinful life, to evangelize her own village. He gathered ordinary men and women around him and entrusted extraordinary revelations to them. As Jesus' disciple, Mary was intimately united with the passion of this first mission. She shared his zeal and lived in the integrity of his fidelity to God.

Priest

This fidelity cost Jesus his life. When the time came for Jesus to bear intense hatred, he refused to respond in kind or to defend himself. At the ultimate test of his message, when his life was threatened, Jesus dismissed the sword, suffered willingly, and died forgiving his enemies.

Mary stayed by Jesus' side during his passion. She followed every painful step to Calvary. Under the cross, she was more than witness. She was offering with him; she was priest. Mary held her son in the faith he needed in his dying on Calvary as truly as she had held him as a baby in Bethlehem and as truly as a priest holds him in Eucharist. As Jesus cried to his Father, "Into your hands I commend my spirit," Mary's own spirit had to be crying, "Into your hands, Father, I commend our son."

The body dying on the cross was her own flesh and blood. At this Eucharist, the paten holding the body of Christ was a rough hewn cross. The chalice holding his blood was the ground where his mother stood. Jesus was both victim and priest, offering and being offered at the same moment. Mary, in her own martyrdom of spirit, was also victim and priest, joined with Jesus in the offering of his own body and blood to God for love of us.

The role of priest is dual—offering and gathering. Mary and Jesus offered themselves and gathered a people in this act of love. It was on Calvary that the Church was instituted, at the moment when the water and blood poured from the pierced side of Christ. Jesus was not alone at this moment. Mary and a few of his followers were with him. Though small in number, this was the Church, the people of God gathered in community to share in the offering of Christ to his Father for the redemption of the world. As sharers in the priesthood of Christ, we continue the responsibility of gathering the people of God into community around Christ.

Scripture has the crucified, dying Jesus committing Mary and John to each other's care. This is our model for Church–compassion and concern for our brothers and sisters in the presence of Jesus.

Guide to the early Church

Mary's responsibility to her son did not end on Calvary. She continued to do his work in his nascent Church. After Jesus' death, the only gospel mention of Mary is the reference to her presence with the Apostles on Pentecost. It is sufficient. Out of love for her Son and fidelity to his mission, Mary would have poured all her energies into his struggling Church. These were the men and women who followed and loved her son. Some had stayed close until the end, like Mary of Magdala. Some ran away frightened like Peter, but they later returned more in love than before. The Spirit was at work again.

Years earlier, the Spirit had come and overshadowed Mary in Galilee, causing Jesus to be conceived. The Spirit descended on the young man Jesus as he began his public ministry. On Tabor the Spirit witnessed to Jesus divinity. And now the Spirit again descends, just as the Church is beginning life in the public sphere. It is fitting that Mary be there to continue her unique call of giving life to Christ. First she gave Jesus her flesh and blood and now she gives the Church of Jesus her support and guidance. It is all the same. The young virgin Mary gave birth to a son. The faithful disciple Mary learned his ways. Mary, the priest, offered the life of her son to God. Mary, Spouse of the Spirit, guided the early Church towards new life in her risen son.

All these expressions are one; they are Mary in abandonment to God and in ministry to the word of God. Mary's mission on this earth was to give life. Her position from eternal life does not change that role. Mary's mission for all eternity is to nurture and foster life for the praise and glory of

God. Gratitude to God for Mary fills us. Gratitude to Mary compels us to set our faces toward life and, in her company, to seek all that fosters life for our brothers and sisters as our act of praise to God.

Mary's Song of Praise

And Mary said,

> "My soul does magnify the Lord,
> I delight in God my Savior
> who looked kindly on lowliness.
>
> Now all ages will call me blessed
> for the Mighty One did great things.
> Holy is God's name;
> mercy is from age to age for those in awe!
>
> The Lord's strong arm did mighty deeds:
> confused the proud in their smug hearts;
> toppled sovereigns from their thrones,
> and exalted humble ones;
> filled the hungering with good things,
> and sent the rich away empty.
>
> The Lord helped servant Israel,
> to remember mercy,
> as was spoken to Abraham
> and his descendants forevermore!"[6]

1. Place yourself with Mary at the Annunciation as she surrenders passionately her entire being, all she is and will ever be. God asks her to be the mother of the Messiah and Mary consents.
2. Allow God to ask the same question of you. "Will you bring Christ into my world?"
3. Let the request consume you until the response arises.

4. Think specifically of what your willingness to bring Christ into your daily life means. Write down these specific expectations of bearing Christ.
5. Stand up and pray the Magnificat, Mary's Song of Praise. Be conscious of Mary praying these same words with you.
6. For one week, begin every day by reading your reflections on bearing Christ and praying the Magnificat.

Chapter Seven

ON BEING SENT

If we accept our vocation to foster life in our time, then we are really accepting to be missioned for the gospel of life. Violence cheapens, threatens, and sometimes destroys life. Faithful to the word of life preached and lived by Jesus, we are compelled to move from merely renouncing violence to actively working for peace. We are compelled to move into the realm of surrender of all things for the sake of the kingdom. This is far more than keeping the commandments, going to Church and not hurting anyone. It involves making a leap from the lived experience of the ordinary person to that level of intimate union usually associated with the saints.

First of all, there is no such creature as the ordinary person. Each individual who is now alive, has ever been alive, or ever will be alive is unique and infinitely valuable in the eyes of God. Secondly, and even more importantly, Jesus came for those who needed him. And those who needed him were very ordinary people. Jesus walked among the simple people of his village and country, many of whom were society's outcasts.

Jesus did not become a learned rabbi, devoting his life on this earth to scholarly pursuits and erudite studies among other learned rabbis. Jesus' father on earth was a carpenter; his mother, a wife and homemaker. When it was time to gather a group of followers to help spread his mission, he chose some fishermen, a tax collector, and an assortment of other laborers. Among his followers were notorious public sinners and timid politicians. Jesus attended weddings, and he cried openly at the death of a friend. He allowed his friend Mary to lavish attention on him and gently taught her sister Martha to just relax and enjoy his company.

Jesus dramatically healed the man who was lowered from the roof in front of a crowd, and he quietly raised a young girl from the dead in the company of only a few. He cured a man who cried out publicly for mercy, and he restored to health a woman who reached out in silence to touch his robe. Jesus cried in frustration when no one in Jerusalem wanted his peace and love. He ate and drank with his disciples and was accused of not being ascetic enough.

Jesus taught from a boat pushed out a bit from the shore; he taught on the side of a hill. He taught in the synagogues and in the streets. His pulpit was the side of a well where his audience was only one person. He did his teaching to one individual after another, to one group after another.

Jesus was at home with lepers and the possessed, with Roman soldiers and broken-hearted mothers. All of these people were at home with Jesus. Children freely approached him. Indeed, when his misguided disciples tried to rescue Jesus from being besieged by the children, Jesus said, "Let the little children come to me, and do not stop them; for it is to such as these that the kingdom of heaven belongs" (Matt 19:14).

As Jesus was one with the poor, simple folk of his day, he is one with every person of our day. Jesus does not change. If his message of redemption was meant for all the people of Galilee, and not just for their religious leaders, then it is meant for all of us, not just those we label "saints."

One of the great contributions of the Second Vatican Council has been to help us realize that the mission of Christ is intended for all the people of God. "For the Christian vocation by its very nature is also a vocation to the apostolate."[7] The work of Christ is our work. We do it as mothers and fathers, business people, lawyers, doctors, car mechanics, teachers, plumbers, bus drivers, actors and artists. Some minister as priests and religious, but their commission to spread the gospel is no greater than that of any other baptized Christian.

But if the call to mission is ours, how do we accept it? How do we prepare to live it? How do we try to love one another in order to praise God? How do we move from renouncing violence to sowing peace?

Spending time with Christ

We begin the same way the people in the gospels began. When they became curious about Jesus they went to see him. They talked to him, asked him where he lived, brought their families to meet him. So, too, we begin by going to Jesus. We might just look at him for a long time to see what he does, or we might start listening to what he says and asking him our questions. Time spent with Jesus is the crucial first step.

We have looked at Jesus as he made his desert decisions for peace. It takes a long time to let the desert experience of Jesus settle in our souls. Those decisions were radically fundamental to his whole message. Being with Jesus in the desert is never meant to be a one-time-only encounter. We need to be with Jesus day after day, as the encounters and experiences of our lives intersect with his, so that we can make our decisions in union with him. As Jesus faced the reality of power and resisted its lure, so must we.

Throughout our lives we are influenced by the hunger for power in our society and within ourselves. With Christ we can be freed from the tentacles that come from the power web. In our personal relations we try living without possessing or controlling. In our businesses we try to live free of monetary gain as our goal. In our social life we risk making decisions that may be politically damaging to our popularity. We begin to see as Jesus saw, in his time of discernment, that many of society's standards are trivial, of no consequence to those who live with God.

Reading the Word

We have seen that this desert time with Jesus is only the first step. We heard him preach the Beatitudes from the hilltop. Do we render Jesus impotent by considering his words inspiring to hear yet impossible to practice? Or do we dare to risk living at the level Jesus did—where the human intercourses with the divine?

We know we are called to live as Christ in our time on earth. How can we even begin to think we are doing that unless we spend time trying to live the message of Christ in the presence of Christ? Certainly we won't understand how to live the Beatitudes from reading the *Wall Street Journal* or *Sports Illustrated*. If the first step in living with Christ is to talk with him, the next logical step would be to read his words. Bible reading hasn't always been a Catholic thing. We all had Bibles; we just didn't open them too often. The Second Vatican Council renewed biblical scholarship and encouraged us to move from merely possessing Bibles to reading them.

There is a priest who has written extensively on spirituality who advocates the "Bible on the Pillow" technique.[8] He suggests that you put a Bible on your pillow—not in your bookcase or on a night stand. When you go to bed, you have to move the Bible. Promise yourself that you will never go to bed without reading one line. Most nights you will read three or four, but you only promise one. When you finish your one line, you put the Bible on your shoes. In the morning when you move the Bible to put your shoes on, you read one more line and then replace the Bible on your pillow. The idea is simple. It takes only a few minutes, but over time it leads to biblical literacy, which can open the door to conversion.

Sharing the sacrifice, sharing the intimacy

Christ goes further than talking to us and giving us a good book to read. He goes beyond just asking us to remember him and his works. Christ brings us to himself in an act of passionate love every time we participate in Eucharist. If we give ourselves over to him at that moment, we dare to enter into his great act of love on Calvary.

Participation in Eucharist on Sundays requires effort if we are to be more than passive pew holders. Eucharist is Christ's great act of surrender and our great opportunity to join him with our own surrender. Such abandonment doesn't happen automatically. Like the woman who insisted that her neighbor get out of bed to give her a loaf of bread in the middle of the night, we need to pursue Christ relentlessly until he leads us to union.

St. Catherine of Siena, a mystic from the fourteenth century, gives us an example of relentless pursuit. She was a passionate young woman with a deep-seated desire to surrender totally to God. And she was a woman who made fierce demands on this God of hers, especially for the good of the Church. She pursued her God relentlessly for renewal of the papacy; and she pursued the pope just as strenuously. Catherine faced opposition at every step of her journey. Sometimes it was from family and friends, sometimes from strangers. Catherine never gave up a project if she thought Christ wanted it accomplished. It was her relationship with Christ that was the strength of her being and her work. Catherine refused to abandon hope that Christ could redeem any situation, no matter how desperate it might seem. Her vibrant, pulsing relationship with Christ and her commitment to the holiness of the people of God led her to the altar every day. It was there at Eucharist that Catherine found her Lord and lover. It was her place of greatest union.

For us this pursuit starts out very simply. We get to Church on time, perhaps even a few minutes early so the sense of rush doesn't accompany us to Mass. We pick up a missalette and glance over the readings to prepare ourselves to receive the Word of God more intensely. We enter into the Mass with song and spirit. We are aware that we share community with the people who are in this sacred moment with us.

Most of us come to Church beset with worries and concerns. The first step in attentiveness to Eucharist is often the conscious laying down of our burdens. We come to the Lord, our God and our lover. We can be ourselves without mask or disguise. We come to praise, to thank, to beseech, to repent, to mourn, to surrender, to be transformed, to eat and drink the Body and Blood of Christ and, finally, to go in peace to carry the word to others.

The experience of Eucharist, when really understood (as much as mystery can be understood), seduces us to want more. Appreciation of Sunday Liturgy can lead us to daily Mass, the best-kept secret in the Catholic Church. If we had even a minute sense of the reality of Eucharist, we would be there as often as possible.

Most Catholics realize that key to the mystery of Eucharist is Calvary. We know it's not a reenactment of Jesus' death; we know it's not a remembering of Jesus' sacrifice. But we aren't quite sure what it is. It is mystery, so explanations are never adequate, but we can clarify. Eucharist brings us present to Jesus as he offers himself to the Father on the cross. It is as if time as we know it is suspended while we are there with him at his greatest moment of surrender. This is what makes us Church—our presence with Christ at this moment of redemption. For us as the people of God, Eucharist is our great moment of unity, when we pray as Church and thus become Church in time and space.

> "The Mass is the only act of worship instituted and authorized by Jesus Christ. When it is not celebrated the church does not pray as a Church; and when the Church does not pray it is in serious trouble.

The Roman Church teaches its members that the Mass is the supreme act of adoration, thanksgiving, atonement, and petition, and the only such act in which the worshipper is ritually united with the entire Church."[9]

Being mission

As Eucharist is by nature union with the whole Church, so relationship with Christ is by nature union with the whole body of Christ on earth. Time with Jesus, time spent reading the Word of God, and time in Eucharist propel us toward our brother and sister in love and in service. What happens to us is what happened to the followers of Jesus in the gospel stories. The person of Jesus attracted people and some of these people became his faithful disciples and apostles. They were able to leave their nets and tax tables because of the strength of Jesus' love for them. In their joy they wanted others to know Jesus. This was evangelization or mission then, and it is the same now.

Often we limit mission to the good works we do in love for others and God. That may be the expression of mission, but it is not the core. The first disciples didn't tell others about Jesus until after they personally knew and loved him. And so, mission is, first of all, union with Christ. It is the experience of intimacy with God through Christ which finds expression in sharing that same love with others.

Witnesses to intimacy, to mission

Some of the world's greatest activists for justice have been our greatest contemplatives: Ignatius of Antioch, the second Bishop of Rome who followed Peter in leadership of the Church and in martyrdom; Francis of Assisi, the 13th-century Italian who turned from an empty life filled with trivial distractions to a passionate commitment to rebuild the Church; Ignatius of Loyola and Theresa of Avila, Spanish mystics of the sixteenth century who dared to reform religious life in Spain at a time when it was dangerous to do so; Brigid and Patrick, fifth-century evangelists of Ireland who lit a fire and began a song of union with Christ which still blazes and resounds today in Eire's sons and daughters.

In our century the witness continues. Dorothy Day, a journalist and pacifist who lived among the poor of New York City for over fifty years, spent her life reading the New Testament and participating in daily Mass. Clothed with justice and yearning for peace, she developed a lay spirituality for our times. Caesar Chavez, an American of Mexican descent who brought fair wages to the migrants working in the vineyards of California, spent from four to five o'clock every morning in prayer with his wife. This was his strength for a life spent pursuing justice for the migrant workers in the United States. Christian lives characterized by extraordinary service to others are lives founded on passionate intimacy with Christ. Activists for peace and justice must primarily be activists for adoration.

Missioned in intimacy

There are many ways we can do good, but we cannot be missioned for Christ until we fall in love with Christ. Gospel missionaries are people like Christ who have no will but God's, no desires but God's, no plans but God's, no means but God's, no message but God's. This was the way Christ lived mission and it is the way we live mission: in passionate intimacy with the Christ who brings us into passionate intimacy with the Father and the Spirit.

We, the not-so-ordinary common folk of our day, are called to this intimacy. We are called to be the disciples of Jesus who go about the countryside and walk the city streets being the mission of Christ. Our mission is Christ's mission— to free the captives, give sight to the blind, open the ears of the deaf, and preach the good news to the poor.

Does this call to mission still seem to demand an extraordinary response which is beyond possibility for most of us? Christianity is always a call to live a paradox. We believe that all is grace; everything that is of God is a free gift of God. We don't earn God's love or ever deserve blessings. Yet we also believe that our response to God is crucial, that how we respond matters to God. His free gift to us does not benefit others until we make it a free gift in turn. With God's help we can do the extraordinary. We live in the time of Incarnation, which means the divine sharing the human and the human sharing the divine. It is mutual gift.

Being part of Christ's mission is a gift from God. It is also the fruit of our own response to God. Christianity is a gift received at Baptism and it is a responsibility to which we give our lives. Passive acceptance of dogma and teachings does not constitute Christianity. Christianity requires effort and attention. If we are afraid that we are not capable of meeting the demands of mission, then we need to go to Christ in love and simply say we are willing to be used. It is not who we are that is so important; it is who we are willing to become. That is what is crucial. One whose being is open to transformation, the believer with a heart willing to be consumed in Christ's love, a person eager to be used for the reign of God—these are the ones Christ will commission. These are the ones who will do great things for God, who will bring Christ's healing grace to a broken world, who will bring Christ's soothing peace to a violent world.

> "Give and it will be given to you. A good measure, pressed down, shaken together, running over, will be put into your lap; for the measure you give will be the measure you get back" (Luke 6:38).

Missioned for the Gospel

As quoted in this chapter, the Second Vatican Council clearly stated the call of every Christian to the work of Christ:

"For the Christian vocation by its very nature is also a vocation to the apostolate."

This prayer is a commitment of time and energy beyond a limited prayer time. Ask God for the grace to persevere in it.

Week One

1. Take out your calendar, your children's activity list, your spouse's engagements—anything that lets you know your commitments of time for this week. In each day find a time for personal prayer.
2. Mark this prayer time for each day this week on your agenda.
3. Take any Gospel—Matthew, Mark, Luke, or John—and begin reading it each day during this prayer time. Ask Christ to enlighten you as to your specific apostolate.
4. Anytime you find yourself drawn to a passage, reflect on it as long as you desire. In the course of the week, you may read only a few lines or you may read the entire gospel.

Week Two

1. Begin again by looking at your schedule for the week ahead. Also check the Mass schedule for churches in your area. Find at least one day when you can participate in Eucharist.
2. Mark this day on your calendar.
3. Go to Eucharist that day to praise and glorify God in Christ. Go to Eucharist that day as part of your apostolate.
4. Ask Christ to unite you with his apostolate of redemption.

Week Three

Repeat Week One

Week Four

Repeat Week Two.

End of the Month

1. What has God spoken to you this month? Hear the words, treasure them. Are they a commitment? If so, be specific as to time, place, preparation, involvement. Write your mission statement—a promise of commitment.
2. Thank God for your call to apostolate.

Chapter Eight

FINDING LIFE IN DEAD BONES

To accept the call to be on mission for the gospel of Christ is to enter into the work of Christ, which is to do his Father's will. This is the kingdom work—to unite with the will of God in gathering all people into one under Christ. The last message of Christ, as revealed in Matthew's gospel, spells out the particulars:

> "Go therefore and make disciples of all nations, baptizing them in the name of the Father and of the Son and of the Holy Spirit, and teaching them to obey everything that I have commanded you. And remember, I am with you always, to the end of the age" (Matt 28:19-20).

Working for the kingdom

For many of us this command seems to be addressed only to those men and women who minister in foreign lands, bringing the Word of God to places that have never heard it before. We must correct this crucial misconception and pray to hear and accept the ministry that we have received at Baptism. Jesus Christ has asked each of us to go to all nations and bring the revelation of God to all peoples.

This is an incredible facet of our faith that cries for response. Jesus didn't ask us just to be good and kind, to say our prayers and give contributions to the poor. All of these things are part of the life of the Christian, but they are not the whole picture. Like Jesus, we must be about the kingdom work, which is much more inclusive.

Inspired but vague on the particulars

A reading of the New Testament shows us the primacy of the kingdom even in the life of Christ. It is interesting to look at these words, written under God's inspiration by people who knew that Jesus was God and that his Incarnation was the fulcrum of all history. Considering this, doesn't it seem strange that so little of the details of Jesus' life and the lives of those around him are recorded? Aside from the birth narratives of Jesus, which are not to be interpreted literally, very few details of Jesus' life are presented until we get to the passion, death, and resurrection. We know almost nothing about Mary, Joseph, and the first thirty years of Jesus' life. We know little of the first twelve apostles, aside from their names, a few of their occupations, and a smattering of conversations.

In today's media this lack of information about famous persons would be inconceivable! Today we want to know everything about the celebrities regardless of why they are famous. If someone is a singer, we want to know not just about their singing career but about every detail of their personality and lifestyle. A sports star becomes a figure in advertising for food, style of dress, cars—all of which have nothing to do with athletic ability. The late Mother Teresa was photographed and deluged by the press whenever she stepped out of her house. Shelves are filled with the biographies and writings of saints who have followed Christ during the past two thousand years. But of the Christ himself, we have very little. A slim volume of stories of healing and compassion, a few pages of teachings, a brief account of a birth and death, a mention of a resurrection—these are the scant details that history has regarding this maker of history.

Part of each of us wishes there were more. Wouldn't we like to know the intimate details of Jesus' life and the lives of his parents and followers? For instance, Joseph remains little more than a name. Wouldn't it be helpful to know how he raised Jesus and something about the relationship between Joseph and Mary? If Peter had a mother-in-law, he had a wife. Wouldn't it be good to know about the first pope's wife and what influence she might have had on Peter and his friends?

All the information we need

We live with our wanderings and wonderings, and we look again at what is given in the gospel. And we believe that everything we need to know is given. Jesus, the Son of God, the Incarnate God, the Redeemer of all creation, did not focus on himself. His focus in life, as revealed in the gospel, is always the will of God. Jesus did not come to glorify himself; he came to glorify God. The details of Jesus' life are important only in that they point to the kingdom of God.

Consumed in kingdom fire

Jesus was consumed with doing God's will and with bringing others to do it as well. Jesus' first disciples learned from their master, and they were consumed with spreading the kingdom of God, not with their own accomplishments. Who they were, where they lived, and what they did were important only in that they were the opportunities for living the kingdom. So when they recorded the stories of their lives, the central theme and recurring details were those of the kingdom.

Mary's primary role was to give birth to Jesus, who would bring the kingdom of God to the people. Joseph's role was to care for Mary and nurture Jesus so they could do the Father's will. In a sense we do not need to know anything else about Mary and Joseph. What we do know is that they found in the details of their own lives concrete ways of responding to the will of God. The details were unique to their circumstances and calling. What we need are not the details but the same sense of abandonment to the will of God and the same urgency of commitment to the kingdom which characterized their lives.

Only one will: God's

Scripture leads us to ponder a paradox, one that requires serious reflection. The details of our lives are absolutely essential to the kingdom and essentially trivial to the kingdom. What we do every moment of the day matters infinitely to God and the work of God on earth; and all that ultimately matters is that the will of God be realized in all places and at all times. We express the kingdom in specific, concrete ways, but it is the response of love behind the act which is crucial, not the specific action itself.

As theoretical as this reflection seems, it is eminently practical. It requires a shift from focusing on ourselves to focusing on God, from what we want to what God desires. It leads us beyond doing good and serving others to doing everything because it is the will of God. We leap from being people who try to live in peace with one another to people committed to the kingdom of peace because it is God's will.

St. Bernard says it clearly: "No longer do we consider what is the will of God for us, but rather what it is in itself. For our life is in his will, thus we are convinced that what is according to his will is in every way more advantageous and fitting for us."[10] This is how Jesus lived. Jesus Christ was so in love with his Father that he lived only for him—this is the experience of kingdom. When we respond to being loved by God to the degree that we are consumed by God's love, then we will be kingdom seekers. Then we will be going out to all the nations, baptizing and proclaiming the presence of God in our midst.

God is God

Once convinced of our commissioning as apostles of the kingdom, we must take the next step in faith and believe that what God desires God will bring to fulfillment. We must believe that the will of God will be realized; we must believe that the ways of God are viable and attainable, that all nations can hear and respond to the word of God, that all people are capable of living in peace. Such belief is lived not by pronouncements of creeds but by decisions made and actions taken in the details of our lives.

For example, if we believe Jesus wants us to love our enemies, we will choose not to take revenge when someone slanders us. We will choose not to defame the reputation of the one who gossiped about us.

If we believe Jesus when he tells us the greatest commandment is to love God above all else, then we will be willing to let go of a high-paying job if it conflicts with the ways of God. If we believe a loving God will judge us on the love we have shown in feeding the hungry and giving drink to the thirsty, then the care of the poor will become part of our daily lives.

Get the mountains moving

Time and time again Jesus told his disciples of the power they would have if they only believed that God will accomplish what God designs and desires.

> "For truly I tell you, if you have faith the size of a mustard seed, you will say to this mountain, 'Move from here to there,' and it will move; and nothing will be impossible for you" (Matt 17:20).

In all the gospel narratives of healing, Christ always gives credit not to his own powers as God, but to the faith of the individuals involved in the healing.

And to the centurion Jesus said, "Go; let it be done for you according to your faith." And the servant was healed in that hour (Matt 8:13).

Then Jesus answered her, "Woman, great is your faith! Let it be done for you as you wish." And her daughter was healed instantly (Matt 15:28).

But Jesus said, "Someone touched me; for I noticed that power had gone out from me." When the woman saw that she could not remain hidden, she came trembling; and falling down before him, she declared in the presence of all the people why she had touched him, and how she had been immediately healed. He said to her, "Daughter, your faith has made you well; go in peace" (Luke 8:46-48).

As these gospel people who met Jesus face to face grew in faith, so also did his apostles who witnessed these healings and heard Jesus' acknowledgment of the faith involved in them. Peter, the same apostle who wavered in walking on the Sea of Galilee and in his staying power at the time of Christ's arrest, learned that all things could be done in Jesus' name.

But Peter said, "I have no silver or gold, but what I have I give you; in the name of Jesus Christ of Nazareth, stand up and walk" (Acts 3:6).

The gospel accentuates the power of faith. Faith has the power to heal and to convert, to strengthen and to sustain. Jesus offers a new way of living, which is far more than the healing of illnesses. And Jesus in the gospel is saying that it is possible to live this way. When Jesus says, "Whatever you ask for in prayer, believe that you have received it, and it will be yours" (Mark 11:24), he is not assuring us that we will get everything we desire. We all know from experience that prayer doesn't work like a mail-order catalogue. But when we surrender our own desires and needs to the will of God and pray for that, then we know that what God wants will be done.

Prayers for peace?

So how do we explain war and domestic violence when we know people of good faith have prayed unceasingly for peace? We cannot explain evil, which is what violence is. We only know that it is not the will of God. And we know that the final word on this earth will be God's word of love. Prayers will be answered as they conform to this word of love. Prayers will not always be answered by the direct intervention of God. God will never use force, even to attain peace. God will respond to our prayers by seducing us to live in peace and love with God and with each other. Peace isn't a fast-food commodity to be dished out through the check-out window at church. It is a gift that we receive slowly, not because God is niggardly in giving but because we are slow in opening ourselves to it. For God to answer our prayers for peace demands that we learn a new way of living and choosing.

A new way of measuring

No longer do we ask whether something is allowed by society's norms, but whether it accords with the will of God as we can best discern it from the life and teachings of Jesus. Society allows us to be violent in sports and in entertainment, but is such behavior consistent with the will of God? We are allowed to murder in the name of the state when we go to war or execute an alleged criminal, but is either action in accord with the teachings of Jesus? It is legal to obtain an abortion and to evict impoverished people from a rental house, but is either action in line with the morality of Jesus?

Every action of our day, in our family, social, and business dealings, has only one measure and that measure is the Incarnate Word of God. The practice of society is to dismiss such a measure as unreal, fanatical. But look at the result of following the standards of society. Is the abandonment of our young to the lessons of a violent media a more effective way to prepare them for life? We think nothing of dropping off a carful of early adolescents to wander a mall, feeding their sense of materialism and consumerism, rather than dropping them off at a soup kitchen or a day-care center to help out. Our thinking isn't straight because our fundamental belief in the primacy of the will of God is weak. We disassociate daily life from the will of God. In the details of each day God rarely rates a consideration. By our concrete actions we show that we often dismiss God as irrelevant, although few of us would dare admit that. God is one of our concerns but usually not high on our priority list if we measure priority by the time and attention we give to something or someone.

If we seldom have the experience of giving primacy to God, we will rarely know the power of God. We will continue to wander aimlessly through the world's fears without the consolation of knowing that God is in our midst and that the ways of God will come to pass if we cooperate.

Dem bones will rise again

In a way we are like the people to whom Ezekiel preached in the time before Christ. We are wandering among the dead bones of violence and despair and we are paralyzed. Just as Ezekiel told his people that those bones would rattle again with life, so our God promises resurrection.

> The hand of the LORD came upon me, and he brought me out by the spirit of the LORD and set me down in the middle of a valley; it was full with bones. He led me all around them; there were very many lying in the valley, and they were very dry. He said to me, "Mortal, can these bones live?" I answered, "O Lord GOD, you know." Then he said to me, "Prophesy to these bones, and say to them: O dry bones, hear the word of the LORD. Thus says the Lord GOD to these bones: I will cause breath to enter you, and you shall live. I will lay sinews on you, and will cause flesh to come upon you, and cover you with skin, and put

breath in you, and you shall live; and you shall know that I am the LORD."

So I prophesied as I had been commanded; and as I prophesied, suddenly there was a noise, a rattling, and the bones came together, bone to its bone. I looked, and there were sinews on them, and flesh had come upon them, and skin had covered them; but there was no breath in them. Then he said to me, "Prophesy to the breath, prophesy, mortal, and say to the breath: Thus says the Lord GOD: Come from the four winds, O breath, and breathe upon these slain, that they may live." I prophesied as he commanded me, and the breath came into them, and they lived, and stood on their feet, a vast multitude (Ezek 37:1-10).

Ezekiel gives us a great story. Being the inspired word of God, it must be more than a fable or metaphor. It prepares the way for resurrection. It challenges hopelessness and despair regardless of the futility of the circumstances.

If Ezekiel were writing in our day, he might see the killing fields of war or the ghettos of violence in our cities and homes as the pile of dead bones. We know the statistics of violence; they are constantly in newspapers and on television. What we don't know is what would happen if we took Christ at his word and tried loving our enemy and returning good for evil. We don't know what would happen if we let the breath of the Spirit blow new life into us and through us into our surroundings. We have deprived ourselves of the grace of resurrection because we won't try any way except that of the retaliatory violence which has led us to this abysmal situation in the first place. Perhaps we cannot even imagine our cold dead hearts living again in love and grace in the presence of God.

Bone-raisers among us

In our day we have seen with our own eyes people who have dared the dead bones of oppression and hatred to rise into liberation and love. Dressed in homespun cloth and sandals, armed with love of his enemies, Mohandas K. Gandhi freed his country of the oppression of the British without ever resorting to violence or hatred. He promised the British they would leave India voluntarily as friends and they did.

Martin Luther King, Jr. taught an abused people to love their oppressors. He resisted the tyranny of prejudice and he did it without hatred or resentment. Dr. King gave his energy and life for the equality of all people, not just the African-Americans. Toward the end of his life, speaking in opposition to the Vietnam War, he was cautioned by his followers that the War was the white man's problem and that getting involved would undermine the civil rights movement. Dr. King refused the warning. Justice was justice and the color of one's skin was immaterial in the search for justice. Dr. King picked up any injustice and held it before the people as a challenge. He refused to let the dead bones of prejudice bury the search for truth.

Archbishop Oscar Romero, a martyr for justice in his native El Salvador, spoke fearlessly and continuously against the oppression and slaughter of his people by their own leaders and military. Against overwhelming odds, Archbishop Romero spoke as a brother to those committing the atrocities. He told them he loved them and he asked them to lay down their guns. He literally looked down the barrels of their rifles. He feared neither death nor torture. Zeal for the kingdom kept him addressing dry souls and hardened hearts and appealing to their potential to love and be loved. A vision of a kingdom of peace and love in his country and in his day fed Archbishop Romero's hope and persistence. He believed the ways of God were possible. And he professed that even his own death would not be a defeat. God would free the people.

A kingdom prayer

It helps now and then, to step back and take the long view.
  The Kingdom is not only beyond our efforts,
    it is even beyond our vision.

We accomplish in our lifetime only a tiny fraction of the
    magnificent enterprise that is God's work.
Nothing we do is complete,
    which is another way of saying that
    the Kingdom always lies beyond us.

No statement says all that should be said.
No prayer fully expresses our faith.
No confession brings perfection.
No pastoral visit brings wholeness.
No program accomplishes the church's mission.
No set of goals and objectives includes everything.

This is what we are about.
We plant the seeds that one day will grow.
We water seeds already planted,
    knowing that they hold future promise.
We lay foundations that will need further development.
We provide yeast that produces effects far beyond our
    capabilities.

We cannot do everything,
    and there is a sense of liberation in realizing that.
This enables us to do something,
    and to do it very well.

It may be incomplete.
    but it is a beginning,
    a step along the way,
    an opportunity for the Lord's grace to enter
    and do the rest.

We may never see the end results,
    but that is the difference
    between the master builder and the worker.
We are workers, not master builders;
    ministers, not messiahs.
We are prophets of a future that is not our own. Amen[11]

Not everyone is as articulate as Archbishop Romero, but
kingdom people are in every walk of life and in every country

and situation. They are recognized by their joy and enthusiasm. A Franciscan priest in Bosnia witnessed the murder of two of his students. When speaking about it, he proclaimed, "There is a side for laughter and a side for tears. Tell them in America that we forgive, that we [Serbs, Croats, Muslims] will live together again. We will be one people. We will forgive."[12] At the time this priest was speaking, political analysts were giving no credence to the possibility that the people in the former Yugoslavia would ever live as one again. All the world looked on the situation as a pile of dead bones that could only be buried in separate burial grounds in separate parts of the city or even in separate cities, according to the religion of the dead person. The kingdom seeker knew the possibility of unity and life; the Spirit of love and hope was only a breath away.

When Mother Teresa was inspired to begin her work among the dying of Calcutta, she was criticized for wasting time on those who were going to die anyway. She was told that the energy could be spent more profitably on the living. Mother Teresa picked up the destitute who were dying in the slums of India. Most had only hours or days before their death. She refused to step over almost dead bones. She saw eternal life in each face, not limited by the earthly measure of life and death. She knew a moment of love was worth more than years of efficiency. She cradled the breath of life until it met the breath of God as she led the poor into the kingdom of God, a kingdom which begins here and continues in eternity.

Welcome the children

A young boy in a residential school for emotionally fragile children had a history of frightening physical and psychological abuse. At times he himself became violent because of the trauma of his life. At Christmas, the school had a policy that the children could not receive presents which glorified violence, such as toy guns or violent video games. The children didn't object because they received great presents, more entertaining than the violent ones. Shortly after Christmas, this young boy told a teacher that he was a peacemaker. Considering his behavior the teacher was intrigued and asked him how? He explained how he thought about the fact that no toy guns were allowed. He had a super water gun which he had purchased for himself after saving allowance money for a month. Without telling anyone, he decided to break up the gun and throw it away. This child would not have understood any attempt at an explanation of the kingdom of peace and justice as promised by God and exemplified by Jesus Christ. But, in the midst of a life of violence and abuse, he took a stand against violence in his own style of play. His actions showed tremendous personal integrity. One person, a young battered adolescent, made a decision against violence in the sphere in which he operated.

Rattle those chains

The kingdom is not an abstract place; it is an event that happens wherever someone chooses life over death. Any choice for the ways of God is an occasion and place for the kingdom. A prison cell or a rural shack can be a kingdom place as much as a monastery or a Catholic school. Homes and businesses are kingdom settings. If we cannot find the kingdom in the supermarket or in the midst of a large family then we will not find it in a church or confessional.

Sr. Helen Prejean was about the kingdom in a poor housing project in New Orleans when God led her to expand the kingdom walls to include death row in the Louisiana prison. The film of her book, *Dead Man Walking,* brought to the attention of the movie-viewing public her experience of life among convicted criminals whom society had thrown away. Sr. Helen worked with individuals who were literally about to become dead bones by order of the state. She talked and prayed with some who seemed to be already dead on the inside. She condemned none; she saw all as children of God, regardless of the evil they may have perpetrated. Sr. Helen is not naive; she knows experientially that forgiveness is a choice made over and over. "Forgiveness is never going to be easy. Each day it must be prayed for and struggled for and won."[13] Whenever people pray this way, the kingdom of God is present.

Prison has never been a barrier to the kingdom. From the New Testament, we hear of the joy and hope of Peter and Paul and all the followers of Christ who sang in chains. The kingdom of God was preached and lived behind the walls, locks and guards. Maximillian Kolbe, a Polish priest, continued his missionary work while a prisoner in Auschwitz, even to giving the final example of love when he switched places with a condemned man and died in his place. Edith Stein, also an Auschwitz victim, spent the few days before her death caring for the children. Chains cannot bind the heart and limit the kingdom.

More recently, a group of hostages from Lebanon came forth from their captivity like Lazarus with forgiveness for their enemies on their lips. Terry Anderson, the longest-held hostage (1986–1991), referred to the hostage group as the Church of the Locked Door. Fr. Lawrence Martin Jenco was one of this group. His gentle, loving God stayed close through turmoil, fear, and the temptation to despair. Fr. Jenco loved his captors, forgave them their sins, and asked them to forgive him his. One of the beautiful stories he told after his release was of a day at the end of his captivity when his guard Sayeed apologized for what he had done to him and asked Fr. Jenco to forgive him. The words overwhelmed Fr. Jenco and he realized he was being called to forgive unconditionally. And he did, but he then said to his young guard, "Sayeed, there were times when I hated you. I was filled with anger and revenge for what you did to me and my brothers. But Jesus said on a mountain top that I was not to hate you.

I was to love you. Sayeed, I need to ask God's forgiveness and yours."[14]

God's will was being done in basement rooms in Lebanon. The search for the kingdom and the fidelity to live it was kept alive by prayer and charity. The same means are available to us—we can pray for our enemies and we can try forgiving them. In doing this we are building the kingdom. God is God but the work of establishing the kingdom of God on this earth is in our hands. For a Christian, kingdom work is not an option; it is the fiber of our being. Our gentle, loving God is present but the work of bringing the kingdom to this earth is entrusted to us.

Morning Prayer of Kingdom Workers

> Go therefore and make disciples of all nations, baptizing them in the name of the Father and of the Son and of the Holy Spirit, and teaching them to obey everything that I have commanded you. And remember, I am with you always, to the end of the age (Matt 28:19-20).

Pray this prayer upon awakening. (A cup of coffee or tea may be an asset.)

1. Conscious of God's presence, light a candle. Praise God for the sun, moon, stars—nature's light. Praise God for Jesus Christ, the light of the world.
2. Thank Christ for the call to be his disciple. Ask him to be with you this day.
3. Reflect gently on your mission to bring others to Christ.
4. Reverently make the Sign of the Cross as a sacred symbol of your acceptance of this mission.
5. Go through your day—hour by hour—anticipating how you will bring about the kingdom this day. Ask Christ to accompany you at every step.

6. As a sign of gratitude to Christ for his abiding presence, wear or carry some sign of your consecration to Christ today—a cross, a ring, a medal, rosary beads. Anytime you notice the symbol during the day, let it be a reminder of your responsibility and gift to be a kingdom maker.

Chapter Nine

CONSCIENCE: A RARE COMMODITY

The world today doesn't seem to reflect the fact that every Christian is called to be missioned for the gospel. Even in countries that are predominantly Christian, it's hard to find the kingdom values being lived. It is often difficult to distinguish Church values from society's values, and that's not because society has become Godlike. Through the centuries Christians have compromised and prostituted gospel values and have surrendered to ways that are not Christ's. Such choices have left us a legacy of mediocrity, half-truths, and lies that parade as Christianity.

In such a non-gospel environment, how does a person who is missioned for the gospel live? How does an individual know what to believe and how to live faith in daily life? How do we distinguish right from wrong?

A surge toward fundamentalism misleads many into believing that answers to the issues facing us today are clear and explicit and that a return to the glorified past is all that is needed. It is not that simple. The past does not give answers today any more than it gave answers to those who lived then. Easy solutions to complex questions only cloud an already confusing area of concern over values and decisions.

The serious issue at stake here is that of conscience and conscience-formation. Moral choices cannot be made in the absence of a well-formed conscience. And the formation of conscience is in critical condition today. We need to bring it into the intensive care unit of our theology to allow it to recover and to thrive again within the individual Christian.

The obligation to search

As soon as the discussion on conscience comes up, warning lights flash for many. The shouts are loud: "Just do what the Church says. That is enough for any good Catholic." It isn't. Sometimes the Church, which is an institution of sinful individuals, is in error in its proclamations; and sometimes the Church is in error by its silence. The Church was wrong when it condemned Galileo and his scientific teachings about the shape of the earth. The Church was wrong in not condemning the Hitler regime earlier. Catholics who believed Galileo were still faithful to their Church; and Catholics who refused to serve under Hitler were faithful to their Church. Those who followed the Church blindly in either instance were responsible before God for the dictates of their own conscience. But blind obedience is not always holy and can be sinful. We cannot fall back on the excuse that we didn't know any better in a particular instance if we have not taken the opportunity to investigate and search for truth.

We are on a very serious path here, and there are obstacles that can hinder us in the journey toward conscience formation. The fear of being wrong or of being alone are two of the risks. Another is that of setting ourselves up as the sole determining standard for right and wrong, which is just as much an aberration of conscience as chosen blindness. A fourth risk is the path of continuing to do evil just because the Church has not yet said it is wrong. That is as harmful as continuing in evil just because the state has said it is legal.

Neither the state nor the Church can substitute for conscience, so risk taking is necessary.

Conscience formation

In her teachings the Church has always upheld the primacy of conscience, but she has not promoted the primacy of conscience formation. This has been a critical mistake, whether deliberate or not, and Catholic behavior mirrors the neglect. It is not sufficient to have profound truth buried within Church teachings. The truths must get into the lives of Catholics in all economic and social circumstances, and for this to happen people need to learn how to apply these truths to their own situation. Conscience formation belongs in the barrios and in the universities, in the Sunday sermons and in the CCD classes, in the sacramental preparations and in the formation of priests and religious. It needs to be part of the faith tradition in emerging countries and in established nations.

Personal choices and decisions which come from a well-formed conscience are the basis of the Christian response to the gospel. It is conscience that molds our response. To fail to form our conscience is to limit our ability to respond.

Conscience formation may appear remote from the reality of daily life for people, since most are too busy surviving to spend hours forming their consciences. But it is the very failure of many to form their consciences which is actually making their lives more difficult.

All who suffer the daily terrors of living in war are suffering because others are following the orders of the state rather than the dictates of a gospel-formed conscience. How else can we explain wars in which Christians are killing other Christians? How can we explain why millions of Catholics fail to love their enemies? How can we Catholics continue to justify living in luxury while others die of hunger and poverty? Conscience formation is indeed practical and needs to be immersed in the daily life of each individual.

Myth vs. truth

In the process of conscience formation, we begin with an honest look at myth-building and myth-breaking. We refer here specifically to the reporting of history which often impacts upon our decisions. It is always the victor who writes the history book after the war. While there is usually some truth in this, there is also some distortion. Over the years some of these untruths or half truths become part of a myth surrounding an actual historical event. Unfortunately, the myths then become the basis for future decisions.

An example of this is the way the American Revolutionary War is usually presented. We have a myth that presents a group of people leaving persecution in Europe. They unite and eventually rebel against British oppression. There is some truth to that. What is not usually taught is the fact that many groups in America, such as the Quakers in Massachusetts or the Baptists in Virginia, continued to suffer persecution from other immigrants who themselves were fleeing religious persecution. What is not usually taught is that there were clear economic class distinctions and that the wealthy Americans who supported the revolution gained a great deal financially. What is not usually taught is that many poorer Americans were pressured into the army against their will. All of these facts are part of the American Revolution, not just the patriotic uprising that can obscure every other issue. The myth of freedom overshadows the facts.

As another example, the reporting of any war suffers the bias of the writers. Often it takes generations before the truth can be spoken honestly and accepted without emotional denial from those who were involved. Historians are still trying to present the facts behind the presidential decision to drop the atomic bombs on Japan at the end of World War II. There is concrete evidence that these bombs were unnecessary to end the war. But the question still cannot be discussed rationally. In 1995, an attempt to present the bombs' effect on Japan cost the Smithsonian Institute its credibility and the director his job. Public outrage at pictures of victims in Hiroshima and Nagasaki was so strong that the exhibit was radically changed. Those responsible for the initial planning were fired. A newspaper editor remarked that it will take another generation before we can admit the reality behind the bombs. The myth of the bombs being necessary to save American lives blocks any admission of the possibility of error.

Twenty years after the Vietnam War, former Secretary of Defense Robert McNamara said he told Congress in 1967 that the war was impossible to win and futile to continue. Nothing was done; the war continued until 1974. In horror we consider the death and destruction that took place between 1967 and 1974. Americans and Vietnamese are still burdened with the physical damage, the psychological scars, and the financial debt of those years. In this case, the myth of fighting against communism blurred the reality of military deceit and political collusion.

During the two hundred years between the American Revolution and the Vietnam War, the Constitution of the United States was the law of the land, and it still is. Yet many Native Americans, Japanese-Americans, Mexican-Americans, and African-Americans have not experienced the right to "life, liberty, and the pursuit of happiness." The myth of equality breaks down before the horrible reality of prejudice and rights denied, past and present.

These examples are from a few centuries of American history. But every country has its own myths and distorted versions of reality. Japan lied about what went on in China; China lied about Taiwan; Vietnam lied about Laos; Laos lied about Cambodia. No country is blameless and no country acts with integrity at all times.

The myth of a caring government

Applicable to all people and all countries is the myth that elected leaders act for the good of the people. Very few men or women today would publicly support this myth, yet most of us continue to act out of it. We continue to do what our leaders tell us to do, even though we do not trust them. If they want a war, we wage it. If they want to eliminate programs which help people get out of poverty, we let them. Wealthy special interest groups seem to get what they need from government while the poor have no voice.

Examples of leaders who lied for personal gain are endless. Some lie for financial benefits and others for political purposes. In the years immediately following World War II, men and women in the armed forces were used as human guinea pigs for experimental nuclear testing. Not only was this truth submerged, but anyone who tried to reveal it was discredited and dismissed.[15] Today the cover-up is being exposed, but the people who suffered illnesses as a direct result of the testing are still not being treated medically or compensated financially. Many have already died.

After the Vietnam War the issue was Agent Orange. The military denied using it so no military personnel could file medical claims for illnesses and birth defects of their children resulting from Agent Orange. Eventually the truth came out when enough people refused to be silent.

Lies surrounding the Persian Gulf crisis that led to the 1991 war began long before the war. The American ambassador to Iraq told Baghdad that the United States wouldn't interfere with its invasion of Kuwait and then lied about it. A young girl told Congress she was tortured by Iraqi soldiers. The truth was that she was never tortured and was a daughter of a high-ranking Kuwaiti official who was trying to stir up support for American intervention. The media reported that babies in incubators were killed. It was totally fictitious. Yet, these stories stirred public opinion against Iraq and incited us to accept it when we went to war. Ironically, hundreds of thousands of babies then died as a direct result of the war's destruction.

Why do we surrender our own consciences and follow the opinion of political leaders who have not proven themselves to be people of personal integrity or moral virtue? And when young men refuse to fight wars initiated by these leaders, why do we look upon them as unpatriotic or cowardly? Why do we still equate "good Catholics" with "good citizens" who support their country, "right or wrong"? Why do we consider tax resisters extremists or fanatics because they refuse to give financial support to weapons research and war? Why do we think it more rational and reasonable and even Christian to pour money into war than to withhold military taxes? When Henry David Thoreau was in prison for his resistance to the Mexican War in 1845, Ralph Waldo Emerson came to visit him and asked, "Henry, why are you there?" Thoreau responded, "Why are you not here?"[16] Could the same question be asked of us? Is Jesus perhaps the one who is asking it?

The myth of technological improvement

We are responsible for following the dictates of our conscience in far more than the political arena. Another myth is that progress is synonymous with continual advancement in wealth and technology. This myth can have a crippling hold on us. It permeates our media and environment. Anyone who questions whether technological advancement is social progress is dismissed as being backward or out of touch with modern life.

Faster and bigger do not necessarily mean better. Work is rarely satisfying in today's society. Is that progress? Many people work under extreme pressure to perform—which means: to make money for the company. Long hours, frequent relocations of home and family, and impersonal treatment from employers are often the signs of a "good" job with big paychecks. Many professional jobs take people's time and energy from their children and their spouses. At the other end of the labor market, unskilled laborers suffer from inadequate pay and the lack of opportunity to obtain meaningful employment. They usually hold down two jobs and merely eke out an existence. Has the human laborer been sacrificed on the altar of technology?

Television replaces conversation. We depend upon sixty-second news bites from a flashy newscaster for our information. We are forming our consciences in front of the television. Hundreds of studies have shown that the violence on television adversely affects our culture and fosters violence within it. Yet none of these studies have led to a lessening of the amount of violence presented on television. With television's sights and sounds filling many rooms in our homes, where do we find the time and place to make our conscience decisions?

When the Church sins

The public media is not the place where we would expect to form our consciences, but our churches are. Yet our Church can fail us and we can fail her. Sermons on money or on isolated issues such as abortion do not educate us to the whole breadth and depth of theological investigation. The same Ten Commandments which have been around now for thousands of years have been interpreted differently for all of those years. The Beatitudes of Jesus have not changed since they were recorded in the Bible two thousand years ago, yet we still struggle to understand their meaning.

Knowing the laws and precepts isn't enough. No commandment or church can tell us what to do or how to act in every situation for several reasons. First of all, the Church cannot predict every situation we will face. Secondly, the Church is made up of people subject to the influences of their day and, hence, they can be in error. There are some absolutes in our faith and these we believe and follow, but there are many teachings within the Church that are merely the opinion of the people preaching them. It takes a well-formed conscience and solid faith education to distinguish between the two.

The Church has, at times, condoned things which she later condemned, such as slavery and anti-Semitism. We are not a perfect Church; we are a living Church, capable of both wisdom and error. Therefore it is not sufficient blindly to follow current practices simply because the Church has condoned them or not yet condemned them. Living our faith involves the active pursuit of truth on the part of each individual member. We are all the Church and we are all responsible for the tradition of faith that we carry.

One voice of conscience

This pursuit of truth is not limited to the "professionals" in the Church, that is, the clergy, religious, and theologians. Each of us is responsible for applying the gospel to the circumstances of life. A powerful example of a witness to truth came from Nazi Germany in 1941. Franz Jägerstätter was a German Catholic, a young farmer with a wife and two small children. When he was called to serve in the Nazi Army early in the war, he refused. His only reason was that he believed it was against the teachings of Christ to fight for Hitler, an unjust aggressor.

At the time, Franz was serving as the sacristan in his village church. The priest tried to talk him out of his resistance, reminding Franz of his responsibility to his family. The army even offered him a non-combat job, but still he refused. At this early stage of Nazi aggression, bishops and priests throughout Germany were either supporting the war effort or remaining silent. But this uneducated farmer saw more clearly than the bishops and priests and refused to participate in what we now regard as one of the greatest evils of our century.

A few years later, the German bishops would finally speak out publicly against the Third Reich. But when Franz followed his conscience, he stood alone, without support or encouragement from his friends or his Church. He was beheaded on August 9, 1942. He died faithful to his conscience and the gospel. Had he listened to the state or the Church, he would have denied both.[17]

Franz Jägerstätter was a daily communicant and a devout Catholic. He studied and prayed over the Word of God, as did many other Catholics in Germany. In him it bore a costly fruit—a conviction that the war was evil and a death sentence for following that conviction. But he had to be faithful to the insight God gave him.

We cannot help but wonder if there were not others who felt the same uneasy stirrings about the war and yet cooperated with it in various ways. We cannot help but wonder about the thousands of simple people who cooperated in keeping the concentration camps running. Aside from the Nazi soldiers who planned and executed the torture and killing, what of the bakers and train operators and local farmers and builders whose skills were used to construct or maintain the camps? We do not judge, but we must certainly ponder how ordinary people could cooperate with such evil. As the camps began to function, the village people near them must have had an idea of what was going on in them. Franz Jägerstätter could not have been the only Catholic in eastern Europe who sensed the presence of evil.

Silence as sin

In our own day we have been terribly scandalized by the abuse of children by some of our priests, and we have cried in shame at the failure of other priests and bishops to speak out immediately and forcefully against the evil. Some of this silence was due to ignorance and some to cowardice. However, most sexual, physical, and emotional abuse of children takes place in their own homes, and the same silence is maintained by their families and neighbors. For every child who is abused, there are some people who at least suspect that something evil is going on. The myth is that what happens within a family is personal. But this is simply not true when it involves the safety of another person. We are responsible for our brother's or sister's child or spouse. Our neighbor's child is our concern. Even the stranger beating a child or wife in the house next door to us or in the neighboring apartment is our concern.

Job sites are also places where "good people" often remain silent in the presence of injustices. If we know that there are dishonest dealings going on, we are responsible for speaking up. If prejudice or harassment are part of our working environment, we are responsible for addressing the issues. Colleagues may snub us as a result. It may even cost us a job. But fidelity to the truth calls for a high level of personal integrity which often implies an equally high level of personal risk. Fidelity to a good conscience calls for heroic honesty, both with ourselves and with others, in facing every aspect of life.

The hard work of spiritual growth

Perhaps it is this honesty which is the cornerstone of truth. Many individuals pray every day, but not many open themselves in their prayer to continual growth in understanding and commitment. It is easier to fulfill ritual obligations in prayer than it is to engage in the risky business of conversion which leads to radical action.

It may be that the absence of formation in spiritual growth is directly related to the absence of conscience formation. No one can force decisions of conscience. No one can even force the consideration of questions of conscience. But we can encourage people to spiritual growth in general. And this is the groundwork which will empower people to think and act through the issues of their lives in a faith context.

Spiritual growth is the process through which we learn to make personal decisions in the light of faith. A person engaged in this process engages God in dialogue about every detail of life. One sermon or one mission will not provide enough insight or teaching for a whole lifetime of decisions.

Listening to many sermons or attending many missions or prayer services will not be enough. The sheer number of religious observances does not produce a religious person. Jesus told us this when he chided the scribes and Pharisees, the religious leaders of his day, for their outward religious observance and their inner coldness to the ways of God.

> "Woe to you, scribes and Pharisees, hypocrites! You are like whitewashed tombs, which on the outside look beautiful, but inside they are full of the bones of the dead and of all kinds of filth" (Matt 23:27).

More than prayers

Being at the temple daily didn't seem to make the scribes or Pharisees holy or capable of right judgment, mercy, and fidelity; neither will daily observance guarantee this for us. Only when we are cleansed interiorly by a deep honesty before God can we enter into the ways of God. The development of inner honesty in the presence of God and of his Word is the life source that produces people who live their faith. Failure to do this difficult inner work leaves practitioners of empty rituals who are full of "dead bones." The scribes and Pharisees were committed to saying prayers but not to the spiritual growth process which would lead to a combination of right conscience and right action. Faith demands more than the addition of prayers and devotions to a corrupt system. Attendance at Sunday Mass, by itself, does not make a person holy. Prayer breakfasts do not make a government holy. Foul-shot "Hail Marys" do not make a basketball player religious.

Our faith is neither a matter of prayers and devotions nor of rules and regulations. It is a completely new way of life based on the life and teachings of Jesus Christ and on the traditions of the people of God through the ages. Our faith cannot be learned in a catechism or passively accepted on the word of another. Our faith, Jesus told us, is a seed which has to be cultivated and tended. The process of spiritual growth is essential to the seed's growing and bearing fruit.

Another image Jesus used in teaching his radical message was that of the new wine. Jesus warned against trying to put new wine into old wineskins: "And no one puts new wine into old wineskins; otherwise the new wine will burst the skins and will be spilled, and the skins will be destroyed" (Luke 5:37). Trying to teach Christianity to people who are not actively involved in their own process of spiritual growth is like trying to force the new wine of Christ into the wineskins of life as it has always been.

Christianity cannot be adjusted to fit into society. Jesus' way is new and calls for radical conversion of heart, mind, and spirit. Too often we have taught Christianity as if it were a compilation of facts and beliefs that can be memorized and then defended against the claims of false religions. Christianity is a matter of the total surrender of our entire beings—body, mind, will, emotions, desires—to the person of Jesus for the sake of the kingdom.

Teachers of faith

Through the ages there have been people like Ignatius of Loyola or Teresa of Avila who recognized the radical call of the gospel and who led others along the path of discernment and spiritual growth. These great teachers taught people to form their consciences according to the teachings of Christ. And many through the ages have learned from them to journey toward union with God. But the vast majority of Christian people have never been taught to develop their faith, have never been guided into living it more fully.

Everyone is called to a vibrantly active faith. Intelligence, money, and education are not requirements for its growth. If we are gifted intellectually, God will use that gift to guide us. If we have a good education, God will use that. If we are rich,

God will teach us to free ourselves from money in order to deepen our faith. If these are not our gifts, it doesn't make any difference. God can draw us in other ways.

In our day the poor in Central and South America use spiritual growth programs called "communidades de base" or base communities. Many illiterate people are developing strong faith lives and learning to form their consciences by studying scripture and applying it to daily life. They are engaged in a program of spiritual growth which gives them a new strength to speak the truth and, as a consequence, to risk their lives. They have found the inspiration to act courageously for justice and to form communities of mutual support. They have seen clearly that the kingdom of God is inconsistent with oppression and injustice. So they stand for the kingdom against their unjust society.

No Christians need apply–Alleluia!

The style of spiritual-growth programs varies with cultures and individuals. There is no single way to progress in a life of faith. A commitment of time and effort is essential and common to all who undertake a process. God's ways are not our ways, so it would seem logical that it will take time to learn God's ways. Desire for God and the kingdom is the starting point. Active involvement in the search is the way. God will give the increase.

> Then when you call upon me and come and pray to me, I will hear you. When you search for me, you will find me; if you seek me with all your heart, I will let you find me, says the LORD. . . . (Jer 29:12-14).

Living the call to mission implies giving our lives to the search for God and for God's ways on this earth. The pain of our people and the example of Jesus move us to question: Why is evil allowed to continue? Why do Church-going adults cooperate with corruption on a daily basis? Few adult

Christians act according to gospel values on a daily basis. Few adult Christians think the gospel even has a place in daily life. Why? Underdeveloped consciences seem to be behind the absence of personal courage and integrity. And behind this reality is the failure of the teaching Church to lead people in the process of serious spiritual growth through prolonged reflection, study, and prayer, thus opening the way to lives of continual conversion.

All of this can leave us ill at ease in society. Jesus knew this. Before he died, he prayed that we would leave our familiar shores and embark on the kingdom journey.

> "I have given them your word, and the world has hated them because they do not belong to the world, just as I do not belong to the world. I am not asking you to take them out of the world, but I ask you to protect them from the evil one. They do not belong to the world, just as I do not belong to the world. Sanctify them in the truth; your word is truth. As you have sent me into the world, so I have sent them into the world. And for their sakes I sanctify myself, so that they also may be sanctified in truth. I ask not only on behalf of these, but also on behalf of those who will believe in me through their word" (John 17:14-20).

Christians do not belong to this world. Christian consciences cannot be formed by the standards of this world. Christians are called to participate in the transformation of this world, and this call demands a commitment of time and effort. Beyond that, this call demands love.

The Courage of Conscience: Will I? or Won't I? Can I? or Can't I?

> "I have given them your word, and the world has hated them because they do not belong to the world, just as I do not belong to the world. I am not asking you to take them out of the world, but I ask you to protect them from the

evil one. They do not belong to the world, just as I do not belong to the world. Sanctify them in the truth; your word is truth. As you have sent me into the world, so I have sent them into the world. And for their sakes I sanctify myself, so that they also may be sanctified in truth. I ask not only on behalf of these, but also on behalf of those who will believe in me through their word" (John 17:14-20).

1. Get a small notebook and keep it near your bed.
2. Every night for a week, go over your day just before you go to sleep.
3. In particular, carefully look at your business and family life. Ask God to clarify reality in the light of the gospel call to justice and mercy.
4. If anything comes to mind that disturbs you, write it in your notebook. Don't try to sort things out at this point.
5. Thank God for loving you through the day. Leave the notebook in God's care while you sleep.
6. At the end of the week look over what you have written. Pray for honesty to see if God is moving you to make any changes in your life.
7. Be faithful to the calls coming through your daily life. No change is too small to be insignificant. (Sr. Helen Prejean became an internationally recognized advocate for people on death row because she wrote a note to a man in jail.)
8. Continue this process of daily reflection. Recognize the calls to conversion as signs of God's love. Be conscious that conversion is not an accomplishment of character but a surrender of being.

Chapter Ten

THE MYSTERY OF SUFFERING
AND THE EMBRACE OF PASSION

Zeal for mission and commitment to conscience formation will inevitably lead to the need to reflect on suffering. Although suffering is part of everyone's life, those who are actively involved in their own spiritual growth process will need to look seriously at the relationship of suffering with mission and with acts of conscience. The presence of suffering need not hinder the mission nor weaken the resolve to search for truth. Actually, union with the suffering Christ, which is where suffering should lead, is an integral part of a Christian's mission and of personal decisions of conscience.

St. Paul presents suffering as a source of joy for anyone involved in Christ's work. Paul takes us right into suffering as a way of being united with Christ and as a way of bringing salvation to the people. Paul is not merely speaking about learning to accept suffering or to endure suffering. Paul insists that we rejoice in it.

> I am now rejoicing in my sufferings for your sake, and in my flesh I am completing what is lacking in Christ's afflictions for the sake of his body, that is, the church (Col 1:24).

Most of us want to avoid suffering, so this passage from Paul seems incomprehensible. It becomes one of those many passages that we figure are meant exclusively for the few saints among us. But is dangerous to eliminate any part of scripture's message, even if we don't think we are able to live it yet. Christianity is meant for all of us, so it cannot be dismissed as irrelevant to any of us.

Taking on mystery

Suffering is mystery. What do we do in the presence of this mystery? Does a fear of being overwhelmed by human limitations block all divine strivings? Does a brush with the crucified Lord send us running in the other direction? Are there times when the resurrection seems hidden?

Teresa of Avila gave some good advice when she was trying to explain the mystery of union with God. While she cautioned that union was beyond all human understanding, she also reminded us of our gift of reason. "St. Teresa says that intellect and understanding are gifts from God which we ought to use until God leads us from human understanding to divine understanding."[18] In saying this, Teresa is referring to the place of intellect in prayer: use it until God suspends it. However, I think the same principle can be applied to suffering. Use reason to delve into suffering's meaning until God brings us to the level of wordless union where we rejoice in suffering with Christ.

It is possible to use our reason to grapple with suffering as long as we keep in mind that mystery cannot be fully understood by reason alone. To reflect upon suffering in the Christian life is to reflect upon mystery, and God alone can reveal mystery to us. While we acknowledge that understanding suffering is beyond human efforts, yet we know that our efforts to understand it do please God. These efforts invite God to give us a fuller understanding. So, we prepare to

receive the gift of understanding of the mystery of suffering–
both in our lives and in the history of salvation and redemption–by studying it seriously.

The existence of suffering is not in doubt. Everyone experiences it, some more drastically than others. Christians
and non-Christians alike suffer; young and old suffer; the
good and the bad suffer. Common to all humanity is the
presence of pain and suffering in life. Despite suffering's per-
vasive presence it is important to state clearly that suffering
was not in God's original plan. God did not create suffering.
God created a universe peopled with individuals with free
wills. It is by choices made by men and women that suffering
and death are brought into the world.

God was not blind to the pain of the people and chose to
save them from an eternity of suffering. To do this God had
to conquer the evil that brought suffering into the world in
the first place. The way God did this was most extraordinary.
Rather than cancel out free will and force humanity into
being good, God sent Jesus Christ to show people how to be
happy and free. Jesus did this by taking on suffering. His suffering freed us from evil. And his suffering bought total and
complete salvation.

If that is so, then why is there still suffering? If we are
saved from the evil that causes suffering, why are we still
suffering? What does St. Paul mean when he tells us to
make up what is lacking in the suffering of Christ? Now we
touch the deeper mystery: that God's sacrifice involves us.
We not only receive the gift of salvation but we participate
in it. Christ allows us to share in redemption by sharing in
the suffering. Christ does not send suffering or desire it for
us any more than he desired it for himself. The suffering is
the consequence of sin, and God will not take away the free
will that causes sin, since it is the same free will that
chooses love. But Christ shows us the way to turn suffering into glory. He lets us share in the transformation of the
world.

The suffering Jesus

Understanding Jesus' suffering is the key to understanding our own. Our primary and constant focus while meditating on suffering is Jesus Christ in his own sufferings. These are not limited to the passion and death of Jesus. They include all the sufferings he endured in his life on earth. Jesus suffered rejection, denial, and abuse long before he began that last journey to Jerusalem. Jesus was God; he loved as God. He was deeply aware of the misuse of the things and people of God in the world in which he lived. He suffered with his people in their oppression and poverty, in their sin and pain. He knew the beauty to which they had been called, and he cried over the rejection of that beauty.

Jesus also suffers in us, his brothers and sisters, who feel the same devastating effects of evil today. Jesus suffers in our pain. Jesus does not feel it the same way as he felt it while he was physically alive, but he experiences it in and through us, his mystical body. If we desire union with this Jesus, we must be willing to suffer as he does. We cannot pick and choose what part of Jesus' life we wish to share and what part we want to ignore.

When we fall in love with Christ we long to be part of all that he is. We want to be with him when he heals and consoles, when he teaches and blesses, and we want to be with him when he suffers and dies. We do not want anything to separate us from Jesus. Courage to be part of someone else's suffering does not come from heroism, but from love—passionate, abandoned love. Down through the ages many men and women—some canonized and some not, some Catholic and some not—have been so deeply united with Christ that they endured great suffering joyfully. Many even begged for the joy of sharing in the sufferings of Christ. The poor man of Assisi gave words to this concept as he gave flesh to his desires:

My Lord Jesus Christ,
two graces I beg of you

before I die:
the first is that in my lifetime
I may feel, in my soul and in my body,
as far as possible,
that sorrow which you, sweet Jesus,
endured in the hour
of your most bitter passion;
the second is that I may feel in my heart,
as far as possible,
that abundance of love with which you,
Son of God,
were enflamed, so as (to be) willing to endure
so great a passion for us sinners.[19]

Living bodies for sacrifice

The crux of the mystery of the cross is love, not pain.
The choice is for union with Jesus, not for an opportunity to
suffer. The reality is that total union with a crucified Lord implies death to self and participation in the redemption of the
world at personal cost. It is the way of Jesus. When we are
seized by his love, it is our way as well.

> I appeal to you therefore, brothers and sisters, by the mer-
> cies of God, to present your bodies as a living sacrifice,
> holy and acceptable to God, which is your spiritual wor-
> ship (Romans 12:1).

Christ invites us to participate in the work of salvation.
And the invitation is to the whole person, body and soul,
flesh and blood, desires and emotions. We have the opportunity to offer our bodies as living sacrifice.

When the Aztecs first heard of Christianity, they resisted
it for many reasons. Primarily because it was being violently
forced upon them, but also because it was confusing. At that
time the Aztecs believed in human sacrifice, and the missionaries told them this was evil and they couldn't continue the
practice. Yet these same missionaries held up a cross with a

crucified man on it and said he sacrificed himself for their sake. In actuality the meaning behind the cross is no less confusing today; we are just so used to seeing the crucifix that the reality of what it means may be lost to us.

Jesus came to give life but he did so by sacrificing his own. For us to live fully, we must also sacrifice our lives. By the mercy of God we are redeemed, and by the mercy of God our bodies become part of Christ's living sacrifice. Whatever we do, if we are united to the will of God, we are a living sacrifice. Our bodies, in health and in sickness, are the living altar of God's sacrifice.

Bearing the grief of sin

In reflecting on this profound mystery of suffering, we must face the suffering we have caused for ourselves and for others. We must dare to let the illusions of righteousness and integrity be drawn aside and the inner reality of our sinfulness be exposed. We must admit that some of this world's suffering is the result of our own sins.

To admit that we are sinful does not mean that we are totally hopeless when left to our own devices. We have moments of sin and we have moments of grace. As Catholics, we believe in the basic goodness of people as proven by the Incarnation of Jesus Christ. Jesus became human, which is a sign that humanity is intended to be good and is capable of being good. We are created in the image of God, and even sin cannot wipe out that potential for good in all of us.

In fact, it is this positive view of ourselves that gives us the power to acknowledge our sinfulness. Does this sound like double-talk? It isn't. The purpose of admitting our sins is to repent of them. And we will only repent when we are moved by love to realize that we are capable of being good. Knowing how intimately we are loved by God gives us the grace to try not to sin again, to dispel the darkness and to be more open to this passionate love. The admission of sin leading to repentance is really an admission of love, given and received. By contrast, the acknowledgment of sin without the awareness of a loving God leads to despair, both personal and societal.

Judas and Peter give us different responses to similar sins. Both denied Christ—one was premeditated and one was a reaction to fear. Both were faced with their sin at the Last Supper—Jesus told each of them he knew what was to come. Both regretted their actions. Judas admitted publicly he had sinned, but surrendered to despair. Peter wept bitterly but still clung to Christ. Peter accepted the forgiveness of Christ, while Judas thought himself unworthy of it.

> Judas, you see, represents that part of our personality which wants only the love that it can earn and thus control. Peter represents that part of our personality that realizes love is unearnable and therefore surrenders helplessly to a love which is beyond merit, beyond control, beyond manipulation, beyond negotiation, beyond anything but grateful acceptance and—here's the catch: with Jesus there is always a catch—enthusiastic response. Judas thought he was not good enough to respond, so he went out and hanged himself with a rope. Peter knew that he was not good enough to respond but it didn't matter. If you're loved with an absurdly foolish love that is irresistible, "good enough" doesn't compute. Only acceptance and response do, an acceptance which is response and a response which is self-acceptance. We need not hang ourselves with a rope, we need not despair because love, unearnable, is nonetheless given. Love is gift, love is graceful, love is grace. And grace, needless to say, is love. [20]

Seeing is repenting

We sin many times throughout our lives. Sometimes we experience strongly the consequences of our sins. At other times our sins hardly seem to affect either ourselves or anyone else. Those are the most dangerous sins—the subtle ones that creep in and turn us from God almost without our awareness. When God lets us see these hidden sins for what they are, he is giving us an opportunity for healing and growth. The experience of sinfulness is not exactly a pleasant one. We are better at seeing other people's sins; it's much less terrifying than seeing our own. It's easy to see others' sins but painful to be a witness to our own. Christ understood this when he warned us about seeing the sliver in our brother's or sister's eye, while being blind to the beam in our own.

> "Why do you see the speck in your neighbor's eye, but do not notice the log in your own eye? Or how can you say to your neighbor, 'Friend, let me take out the speck in your eye,' when you yourself do not see the log in your own eye? You hypocrite, first take the log out of your own eye, and then you will see clearly to take the speck out of your neighbor's eye" (Luke 6:41-42).

The grace to see the log, to see our sins involves two parts. But we usually see both of these parts simultaneously and this timing makes the grace almost unbearable. The first part is to see ourselves as sinning; the second is to see God as loving. If we had only the first part, the sight of our sins, we would become mired in hopelessness over the evil we have done. If we had only the second part, we would be aware of a loving God but one who was removed from us in our sinfulness. God could be loving but the distance between us would be infinite. To experience both parts at the same time is to realize we have turned our backs on the one who loves us most intimately. This is excruciating pain.

In their writings, many saints reveal the pain they experienced when they faced their own sinfulness in the presence of a loving God. Sometimes it is hard for us to understand what they are talking about because they seemed to be living lives of great virtue and holiness. We tend to disbelieve them and think of them as fanatics. For example, Teresa of Avila wrote about the years before her conversion as times of mediocre virtue. That we can understand. However, Teresa also wrote of the sinfulness of her later years when all outward appearances seemed to point to a life of extraordinary virtue. This we find hard to grasp.

Mohandas K. Gandhi gives us another example. When Gandhi told of his conversion from the life of a middle class lawyer to a poor mendicant, it was clear that he recognized his own self-centeredness and became converted to a more selfless union with God and other people. But at the end of his life, years after his initial conversion, Gandhi admitted his failure to fully impart the philosophy of nonviolence to his people. Now we are confused. We look at a man who fasted almost to death, left aside all personal gain, and offered his life for his people. What more could he have done? It seems as if the more Teresa and Gandhi surrendered themselves to God, the more conscious they became of their failure to surrender! The closer they got to God, the more they saw their sinfulness.

Passionate love

We are struggling here to understand passionate love. We are struggling to understand Jesus' words: "So you also, when you have done all that you were ordered to do, say, 'We are worthless slaves; we have done only what we ought to have done!'" (Luke 17:10).

When Jesus calls us to embrace him as lover, as he calls every Christian, we must be willing to face the inadequacy of our own love. When we deeply offend someone we love, we suffer the pangs of infidelity. If there is to be healing we need to admit our failure and ask forgiveness. If that person whom we have offended has a love great enough, our failure can become a springboard not only for forgiveness but for a newly enflamed passion.

Jesus Christ loves us enough to bear our infidelities. Jesus Christ is love incarnate. He trusts us enough to reveal our sinfulness so we can turn away from sin and embrace him more fully. Sin limits the embrace of God; it keeps us from intercourse with God. Self-knowledge lets us see specific ways in which we block this consummation with Christ. Self-knowledge helps us see how we refuse the love offered us, how we ignore God and resort to actions which deeply offend God.

In a way there is no such thing as a small sin or "venial sin," as it is commonly called. Of course, there is an objective degree of difference among evil acts. However, once we have begun to relate to Jesus Christ personally and intimately, any offense against him is major. Any rejection of the Beloved is intolerable. The cost of passionate love is high. The cost of total abandonment is high.

O happy fault

Part of the cost is bearing responsibility for our sins. When we accept this responsibility, we find ourselves grateful to God for the opportunity to bear it. As painful as it is to admit having rejected our greatest lover, we are grateful to see how we have. We long to be more faithful lovers, so we want to know how we have offended God. We want to repent and not sin again. The gospel woman who was forgiven many sins was not brought to repentance by fear; she was won over by love and in that light saw her many sins. How wonderful of Christ to have loved her into faithfulness! He let her see her sinfulness so she could choose to change. He longs to do the same for us.

God offers us the grace of self-knowledge, the grace to see our sins. God loves us enough to lead us to understand that anytime we have offended another person we have offended God. This is a difficult experience. Most of us sin through lack of thought, weakness, fear, or self-absorption. We seldom think of deliberately denying God. So when we begin to see that all sin is a denial of God, we feel terrible.

We want to express our sorrow. We want to show God that we are sorry. We want God to allow us to suffer the pain of sin so that we can experience in our bodies the penance of sorrow. God exacts no punishments for sin; Jesus Christ took all sin upon himself and conquered all of it. Yet God allows us to make our personal acts of repentance because we need to. Peter denied Christ. Christ forgave Peter unconditionally, but Peter needed to cry in the night. He needed to experience in all its anguish a heart broken by infidelity, a body racked with sorrow.

We also have, by the incredible grace of God, our moments of crying in the night after realizing our denial of Christ. These cries of sorrow turn into cries for resurrection. Cries for mercy become mingled with alleluias. Freely we accept responsibility for our share in sin and freely we receive a share in the redemption from sin. With Christ we die and rise again. "Dying, you destroy our death; rising, you restore our life."

We are saved by love. Knowledge of sinfulness opens us to the depths of Christ's redeeming, consuming love. The willingness to suffer the bitter truth of our own sins is the willingness to die in order to rise to new life in Christ. To receive wings the moth must die in its cocoon. Once our soul has wings, it must fly to God.

> It has wings now: how can it be content to crawl along slowly when it is able to fly? All that it can do for God seems slight by comparison with its desires.[21]

We are released from our sins. We experience an explosion of desire so intense that only God can satisfy it. And God will.

Beyond words

The final word on suffering must be one of compassion and hope. The suffering that people endure because of poverty, oppression, violence, natural disasters, and physical and mental illnesses stirs the heart of Christ. For those experiencing the pain, our God, who is most present to them in that pain, can seem distant or even absent. At these times there are no theories of suffering, no reflections on suffering, no desire to understand suffering. There is only the suffering, so intense it obliterates all other thoughts. Yet in the absence of human hope God comes–presence without words, compassion without limit.

> We suffer, we suffer into truth.
> In our sleep pain that cannot forget falls drop by drop upon the human heart and in our despair, against our will, comes wisdom through the awful grace of God.[22]

Jesus Suffering in Us and for Us

> I am now rejoicing in my sufferings for your sake, and in my flesh I am completing what is lacking in Christ's afflictions for the sake of his body, that is, the church (Col 1:24).

1. For this prayer go to a Church or chapel where the Blessed Sacrament is present.
2. Sit in the presence of God and keep your eyes focused on the tabernacle or cross.
3. Allow the sufferings you have experienced in the past or are presently enduring to gently come into your consciousness. Resist the urge to try to escape them or fear them. Hold them before Christ and say, "Lord, I have suffered for you."
4. When the sufferings have been acknowledged and offered, gaze on the crucifix and allow God to say to you, "And I have suffered for you, (insert your name here)."
5. Allow gratitude to be expressed by both you and Christ.

Chapter Eleven

THE HUNDREDFOLD

As Jesus was setting out on a journey, a man ran up and knelt before him, and asked him, "Good Teacher, what must I do to inherit eternal life?" Jesus said to him, "Why do you call me good? No one is good but God alone. You know the commandments: 'You shall not murder; You shall not commit adultery; You shall not steal; You shall not bear false witness; You shall not defraud; Honor your father and mother.'" He said to him, "Teacher, I have kept all these since my youth." Jesus, looking at him, loved him and said, "You lack one thing; go, sell what you own, and give the money to the poor, and you will have treasure in heaven; then come, follow me." When he heard this, he was shocked and went away grieving, for he had many possessions.

Then Jesus looked around and said to his disciples, "How hard it will be for those who have wealth to enter the kingdom of God!" And the disciples were perplexed at these words. But Jesus said to them again, "Children, how hard it is to enter the kingdom of God! It is easier for a camel to go through the eye of a needle than for someone who is rich to enter the kingdom of God." They were greatly astounded and said to one another, "Then who can be saved?" . . .

Peter began to say to him, "Look, we have left everything and followed you." Jesus said, "Truly I tell you, there is no one who has left house or brothers or sisters or mother or father or children or fields, for my sake and for the sake of the good news, who will not receive a hundredfold now in this age—houses, brothers and sisters, mothers and children, and fields with persecutions—and in the age to come eternal life" (Mark 10:17-26, 28-30).

God's desires and ours

This text used to be a common one for vocation talks for the ordained priesthood or religious life. There was nothing wrong or inappropriate in such use. The error, by omission, was in restricting this preaching of Jesus to only those groups. Jesus didn't teach in a seminary or a novitiate. He taught men and women who labored hard for their survival. They fished and farmed, spun thread and wove garments, baked bread and crafted tools and furniture.

Some of the people in the crowd listening to Jesus were middle class. We know a few were wealthy, but most were poor. The Jewish people were oppressed by Rome and, just like oppressed people today, their lives were difficult. When rights are denied so also is the ability to live comfortably. Oppression and poverty are grafted together at the root.

Jesus was one of these oppressed people, yet he exuded hope and pointed to a different vision. Jesus promised that the reward for fidelity to the ways of God would be great here and hereafter. God will not be bound by the injustices of society; goodness cannot be limited. The range of evil seems to be limitless but Jesus promised that everything freely surrendered for the kingdom will be compensated a hundredfold.

The spark for this teaching on God's bounty is Jesus' encounter with the rich young man. Jesus saw the youth's zeal and the beginning of a fire for God in him, so Jesus called him to a deeper level of intimacy. Jesus tried to fan the spark of desire, the beginning of love. Unfortunately, it was too radical a commitment for the man at the time, so he went away sad. We don't know what happened to him. The gospel only presents an opportunity wasted, a call unheeded.

Jesus also must have been sad. He loved the young man and offered him the way to happiness. Jesus knew riches and possessions have nothing to do with happiness. He was trying to prevent the emptiness that he knew would pursue the wealthy young man as it does all who base their worth and value on wealth. It is almost possible to hear Jesus' sigh when he said, "Children, how hard it is to enter the kingdom of God! It is easier for a camel to go through the eye of a needle than for someone who is rich to enter the kingdom of God."

Jesus knew the deep challenge facing the young man in front of him. Jesus himself faced it in the desert—the lure of economic security as a foundation of life. Because he is God, Jesus knew what gives happiness and what doesn't. If anything or anyone is placed above God there can be no happiness. "What does it profit them if they gain the whole world, but lose or forfeit themselves?" (Luke 9:25)

This dialogue between the young man and Jesus shows their different perspectives. They both had the same goal—to be happy and fulfilled. They had opposing means to achieve the goal—one was abandonment and the other possession. The story ends with sadness in both hearts. The parting is poignant.

Reward time

Others overheard the conversation and wanted more clarity, especially Peter. He understood what was being asked of the young man. Not so long ago the same call was offered Peter and his brother and friends: "Come, follow me." Peter had followed quickly. Peter made mistakes but he never turned back. So he asked the obvious: "What about those of us who have followed?"

Jesus' answer reveals the reward of surrendering everything for the sake of God. To be with God is better than anything this world can offer, even better than all the good things God gives us in this world—the love of a spouse, children, family, friends. Those who surrender all to God find fulfillment.

This is an extraordinary phenomenon. Human relationships can bring great fulfillment through the love of a spouse and children, yet fulfillment can also be realized when beautiful human gifts are abandoned for the sake of the kingdom. Again, our reflection on the gospel leads us into paradox, into mystery.

The rewards Jesus promises are not understandable without faith. On a human scale we usually understand rewards. If we invest in education, we broaden our world view and acquire the skills to earn a wage higher than we would have without the education. That is a reward of education. If we save our money on a regular basis, we can invest it for the future. That is a reward of budgeting. If we care for our bodies with diet and exercise, we have fewer health problems. That is a reward of a healthy lifestyle. If two people invest time and effort in a relationship, it will bear fruit. And on and on we can go with examples from human experience.

Jesus takes human fulfillment to a level only the eyes of faith can see. Jesus knows that the human bond of friend, spouse, or child can develop the human spirit and bring it to a deep level of compassion and love. We grow through our relationship with others; the greater the intimacy, the greater the possibility for growth. Yet Jesus is saying that if we surrender even these beautiful gifts of life for the sake of the kingdom, we are still able to be humanly fulfilled.

When Jesus speaks of giving all for the kingdom he does not mean that only celibate people with vows of poverty and obedience are called to surrender everything. Jesus says to all of us that the kingdom comes first, even before our personal needs. If the job of the main wage-earner in a family compromises Christian values, then the job must be abandoned even at the risk of unemployment. In our day there are people who have taken the risk. Some workers in the defense industry in Connecticut, Texas, and Illinois quit their jobs when they had the grace to see that they were cooperating with violence. A New York accountant who refused to alter the books for a company lost his job. Parents who raise their children to be compassionate and just risk the loss of social status for living the values they profess. History is filled with the stories of courageous individuals who exposed human rights violations at the risk of job and life. Trust in God becomes very concrete when a family's source of income is abandoned for gospel values.

Christianity costs and the price is dear. It demands all that we have and are and ever will be. And the price tag is the same for every Christian. God asks as much of sinners and beginners as of saints and mystics. Our potential for response increases with our choices to love, but at all times God asks all we are capable of giving.

To gain everything we abandon everything, to possess life we surrender life. Total surrender doesn't make sense. But nothing in Christianity is meant only to make sense; the goal of Christianity is to make love.

Ecstasy or survival?

What Jesus is really offering to the rich young man, to Peter, and to us, is the choice between survival and ecstasy. Jesus did not condemn the young man for not making the leap of faith offered him. God will not strike us dead for mediocrity. God allows us to live with our choices. If we settle for survival on a spiritual level, for mere observance of the law, there will be no punishment or divine retribution. But neither will there be ecstasy. The human spark of surrender will not be consumed in the fiery flames of divine passion. Left untended, the fire in the soul's hearth will die and we will be cold. A penetrating chill will invade us. God desires us with divine desire. Why are we so fearful?

It isn't easy to let go of the known for the unknown even if it is what the Christian call requires. If our eyes are focused only on what we hold in our hands, we will never take the risk to reach for what might be beyond our grasp.

Surrender to God doesn't take place in our heads. It doesn't even take place in our hearts. There is a place within us that is the essence of our being. This is where abandonment happens or doesn't. No theory or treatise, no sermon can move us here. In this center only God and the person dwell. In this center all our gifts of mind, body, and spirit can be focused exclusively on God. On God we fix our eyes, eyes wild with desire and passion. Our gaze is riveted on God's gaze, and we are held spellbound by it. The hundredfold flows in the space between eye and eye, heart and heart.

Total surrender to the fire of God's love is the prerequisite. Consummation in love is the hundredfold. The line where surrender stops and consummation begins cannot be drawn. We are one with God and the union is the hundredfold. Even a glimpse of the face of God renders all earthly treasures worthless in the presence of infinite wealth.

God calls us to leave everything and offers us the hundredfold. The offer is made to all of us, not just those "holy" people like John of the Cross or Teresa of Avila. God cannot and does not offer less love to some and more to others. God gives to us a love pressed down and overflowing. God is love, whole and entire, undivided and all-encompassing. If we share even a bit in God we share all.

We become such lovers, mystics by the grace of this God in very ordinary ways. We learn to trust God in day to day matters such as health, food, shelter, friends. When things go awry in our lives we believe that no matter what happens God still loves us and cares for us. If others slander us and destroy our reputations, we cling to God for our only security, knowing that God alone is the judge of all. When our brothers or sisters abuse or insult us, we love in return because the ones hurting us are also children of God. Ecstasies and visions are not the essential stuff of mysticism. Charity practiced faithfully, hope lived in despair, and faith believed beyond intellectual understanding are the backbone and flesh of mystical union with God.

Jesus offers us the kingdom here and now. Through the rich young man, Jesus shows us the first steps toward this eternal, infinite life of fulfillment and peace. We must simply put down the possessions that burden us, share whatever we have with the poor, and stay in the company of Jesus. It isn't complicated, but neither is it easy. And it is the best offer we will ever receive. To surrender and abandon all we have and possess and are, to surrender all we will ever have or possess or be, is to come alive, to dwell in the passionate embrace of God. If two or three of us gather together to do this, fire will come again to this fragile earth of ours. And this fire will burn without consuming. In its wake, in our wake, peace will spring up like crystal clear water to refresh our war-weary world and quench our children's life-thirst for peace.

Jesus challenges us to enter into himself, to explore him intimately. It is the exploration into the unknown God who knows us perfectly and loves us passionately. The quantum leap from unknown to unknowable is before us.

> The human heart can go to the lengths of God.
> Dark and cold we may be, but this
> Is no winter now. The frozen misery
> Of centuries breaks, cracks, begins to move;
> The thunder is the thunder of the floes,
> The thaw, the flood, the upstart Spring.
> Thank God our time is now when wrong
> Comes up to face us everywhere,
> Never to leave us till we take
> The longest stride of soul men [and women] ever took.
> Affairs are now soul size.
> The enterprise
> Is exploration into God.[23]

Of Passion and Folly

Jesus said, "Truly I tell you, there is no one who has left house or brothers or sisters or mother or father or children or fields, for my sake and for the sake of the good news, who will not receive a hundredfold now in this age—houses, brothers and sisters, mothers and children, and fields, with persecutions—and in the age to come eternal life" (Mark 10:29-30).

1. In a quiet place, devoid of distractions, meet with Jesus. See him approaching the rich young man. Listen to their conversation. Watch Jesus and the young seeker as he walks away saddened.
2. Now let Jesus turn his full attention to you. What is he asking you?
3. You have time, so let his request sit in your soul. Is there resistance in you? Is there also eagerness to respond? Are you being asked for a "yes" or for a "no"?
4. Imagine yourself saying "no." To what does it lead you tomorrow?
5. Imagine yourself saying "yes." To what does it lead you tomorrow?
6. Repeat this prayer daily until you are able to make a decision.
7. Celebrate the moment of decision. Either a "yes" or a "no," if they are of God, will be an occasion for joy.

(*A note of caution here:* Be careful not to dismiss simple, relatively minor changes as unimportant. God leads us slowly and gradually. There is no action that is unimportant if it is an occasion of our surrender to God.)

NOTES

1. For greater background on the issue of Rome being trivial to the kingdom of God, see John L. McKenzie, *The Power and the Wisdom* (Milwaukee: The Bruce Publishing Company, 1965) 237–8.

2. e. e. cummings, *Complete Poems* (New York: Harcourt, Brace, & Javanovich, Inc., 1972) #68.

3. Lorraine Hansberry, *A Raisin in the Sun* (New York: Penguin Books, USA Inc., 1988) 145.

4. Thomas Merton, *Gandhi on Non-Violence, A Selection from the Writings of Mahatma Gandhi* (New York: New Directions, 1965) 34.

5. St. John of the Cross, *Dark Night of the Soul,* trans. E. Allison Peers (New York: Image Books, Doubleday and Co., 1959) stanza 8.

6. Joyce Ann Zimmerman, C.PP.S., and others, *Pray Without Ceasing, Prayer for Morning and Evening* (Collegeville: The Liturgical Press, 1992) 27.

7. *Decree on the Apostolate of the Laity,* Second Vatican Council, 1965, #2.

8. Fr. David Knight, Memphis, Tennessee, preaches this suggestion for reading the Bible.

9. John L. McKenzie, S.J., *The Roman Catholic Church* (New York: Holt, Reinhart, Winston, 1969) 187.

10. St. Bernard, *The Liturgy of the Hours,* vol. II (New York: Catholic Book Publishing, 1975) 235–6.

11. James B. Dunning, *Echoing God's Word* (North American Forum on the Catechumenate) 380.

12. Taken from an interview with the author in Bosnia-Herzogovina in June 1996.

13. Sr. Helen Prejean, *Dead Man Walking* (New York: Random House, 1993) 245.

14. Lawrence Martin Jenco, *Bound to Forgive* (South Bend, Ind.: Ave Maria Press, 1995) 14.

15. Carole Gallagher, *American Ground Zero, The Secret Nuclear War* (New York: Random House, 1993); Ted Bartimus and Scott McCartney, *Trinity's Children, Living Along America's Nuclear Highway* (Albuquerque: University of New Mexico Press, 1991).

16. Henry David Thoreau, *On the Duty of Civil Disobedience* (London: Housmans, 1980) 2.

17. Gordan Zahn, *In Solitary Witness, the Life and Death of Franz Jägerstätter* (Boston: Beacon Press, 1968).

18. Teresa of Avila, *Interior Castle,* trans. E. Allison Peers (New York: Image Books, Doubleday and Co., 1961) 89.

19. *The Prayers of St. Francis,* compiled by W. Bader (New York: New City Press, 1994) 34.

20. Andrew Greeley, *Love Song* (New York: Warner Books, Inc., 1989) 439.

21. Teresa of Avila, *Interior Castle,* 107.

22. Aeschylus, *Agamemnon,* trans. Edith Hamilton (New York: W.W. Norton & Co., 1937) #179–84.

23. Christopher Fry, *A Sleep of Prisoners, Three Plays* (New York: Oxford University Press, 1965) 209.